THE VAN BUSKIRKS OF INDIANA

THE VAN BUSKIRKS OF INDIANA

Western Migration from New Netherlands
11 Generations — 1654-2017

EDMUND MICHAEL VAN BUSKIRK

Genealogy House
Amherst, Massachusetts

Copyright 2018 Edmund Michael Van Buskirk
All rights reserved.

Published by Genealogy House, a division of White River Press
PO Box 3561, Amherst, MA 01004

ISBN: 978-1-887043-41-0 (hardcover)
ISBN: 978-1-887043-46-5 (ebook)

Copy Edit by Jean Stone, Martha's Vineyard, MA

Book and Cover Design by Douglas Lufkin, Lufkin Graphic Designs, Norwich, VT 05055

Index by Janet S. Blowney, Boston, MA

Library of Congress Cataloging-in-Publication Data

Names: Buskirk, Edmund Michael Van, 1941-author.
Title: Van Buskirks of Indiana : 11 generations, from Holstein, Denmark to
  New Netherlands and the New World 1654/2017 : generations 1-11 / Edmund
  Michael Van Buskirk.
Description: Amherst, Massachusetts : Genealogy House Publishers, [2018] |
  Includes bibliographical references.
Identifiers: LCCN 2018024576 | ISBN 9781887043410 (hardcover : alk. paper)
Subjects: LCSH: Buskirk, Edmund Michael Van, 1941---Family. | Van Buskirk
  family. | Van Buskirk, Laurens Andriessen, approximately
  1625-1694--Family. | Physicians--United States--Biography. |
  Indiana--Genealogy.
Classification: LCC CS71 .V2217 2018 | DDC 929.20973--dc23
LC record available at https://lccn.loc.gov/2018024576

DEDICATION

To Bette, my wife and soulmate for over 50 years, for her love, ceaseless encouragement, legion proofreading and intrepid support for a multitude of revisions. Our forays together into musty libraries, abandoned graveyards and obscure country roads meander between the printed lines.

To my daughters Audrey, Sarah and Amy, for their encouragement, curiosity, careful editing, apt suggestions and unmitigated love.

To Family. This story begins and ends with family. We are born into family. If we are lucky, we die within family, but family lives on, generation upon generation.

The Van Buskirks of Indiana

MICHAEL VAN BUSKIRK GENERATIONS 11–6

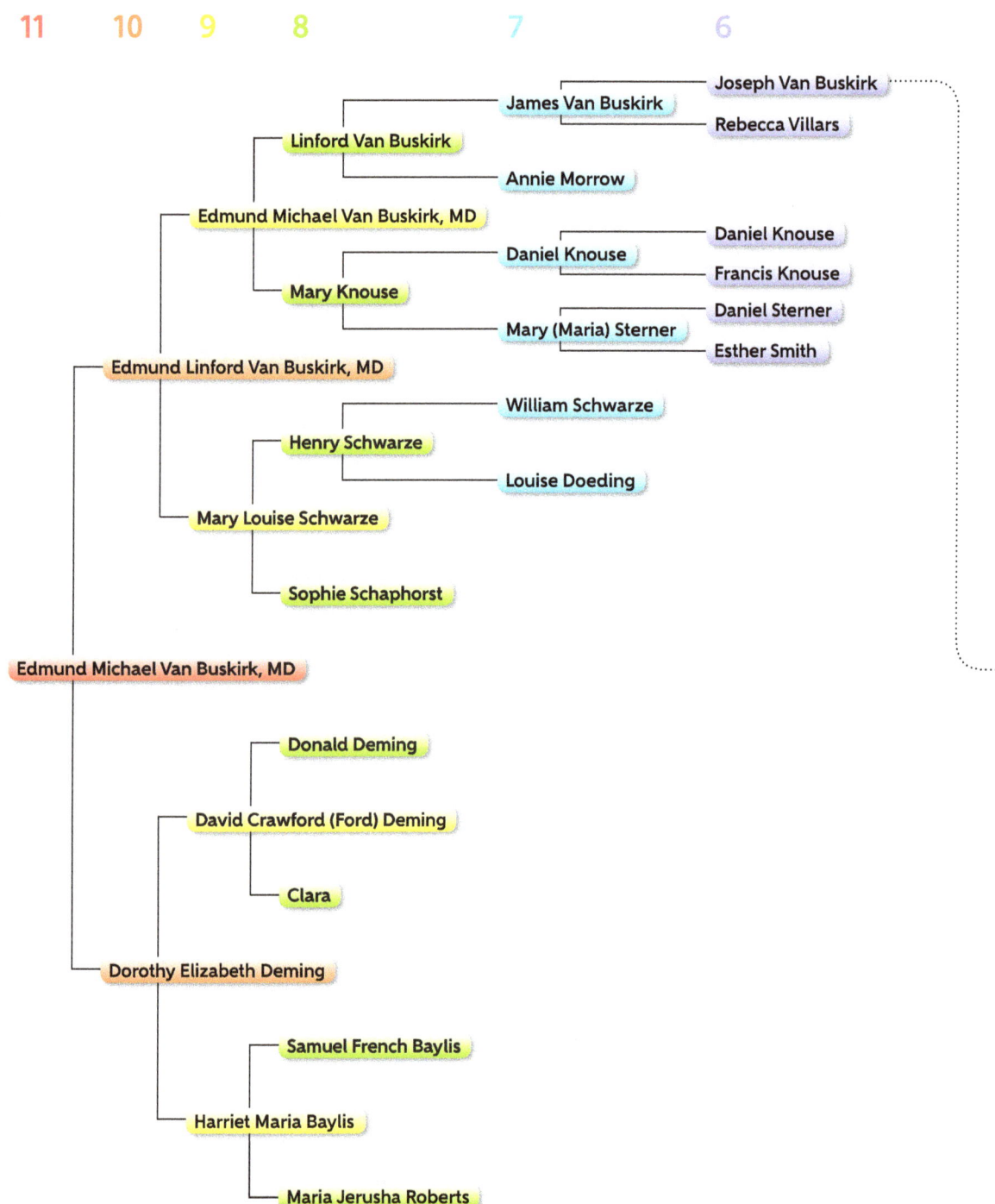

MICHAEL VAN BUSKIRK GENERATIONS 6-1

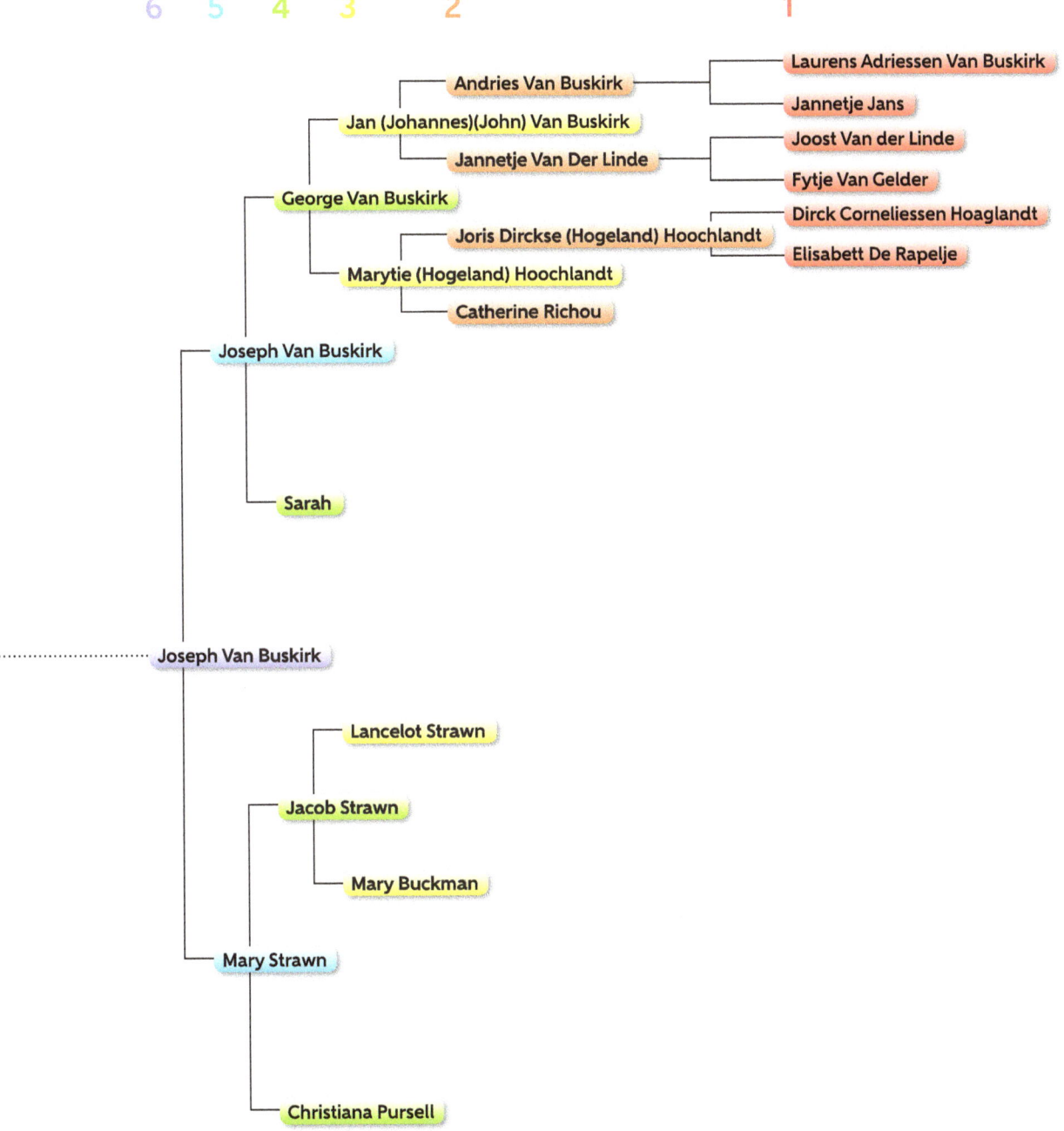

CONTENTS

Figures ix

Portraits xi

Preface xiii

Origins of the Van Buskirk Name 1

Background 3

1. First Generation: The Van Buskirks of North America 9
   Laurens Andriessen Van Buskirk (ca. 1625–1694)

2. Second Generation: Four Sons of Laurens Andriessen Van Buskirk . 18
   Andries, Laurens, Pieter, and Thomas

3. Third Generation: Jan (John) Van Buskirk (ca. 1670s–1730s) 26

4. Fourth Generation: George Van Buskirk (1721–1800) 29

5. The Post-War Westward Migrations 32

6. Fifth Generation: Joseph Van Buskirk (1751–1821) and his Siblings . 42

7. Sixth Generation: Joseph Van Buskirk (1782–1864) 44

8. Pioneer Life in Eastern Ohio 51

9. Seventh Generation: James Van Buskirk (1811–1869) 54

10. Eighth Generation: Linford Van Buskirk (1847–1910) 60

11. Ninth Generation: Edmund Michael Van Buskirk, MD (1875–1950) . 64

12. Tenth Generation: Edmund Linford Van Buskirk, MD (1905–1995) . 73

13. Byways of Distant Cousins 81
    I: The Loyalist

14. Western Migration: The Final Leg on the Oregon Trail 87

15. Byways of Distant Cousins 92
    II: The Van Buskirks on the Oregon Trail

16. Byways of Distant Cousins 104
    III: Captain David Van Buskirk, The Tallest Man in the Union Army

17. Byways of Distant Cousins 109
    IV: The Resurrectionist

18. Eleventh Generation: Edmund Michael Van Buskirk, MD (1941–) .120

Bibliography 135

Appendix 139

Index 149

FIGURES

1. Hudson's Three Rivers 5
2. Holstein to Amsterdam 10
3. Lot 19, Mingackwa Property of Laurens Andriessen Van Buskirk . . 13
4. Laurens Andriessen Van Buskirk properties on 1873 maps 15
5. Van Buskirk properties in 1694 marked on a 1990 map 16
6. Revolutionary War map of Bergen Neck and Constable Hook 21
7. Pieter Van Buskirk, house and tombstone 22
8. Thomas Van Buskirk house 24
9. Combined map of Van Buskirk properties in New Netherlands. . . . 25
10. Wynkoop House built by John[3] Van Buskirk in 1734 28
11. Map of Tenmile Country 34
12. Map possible routes to Tenmile Country 37
13. Possible routes from Tenmile Country to Tuscarawas Valley 48
14. Carroll County, Ohio, Lot 34 49
15. Madison Township, Monroeville Farm, 2002 56
16. Brown's Family Graveyard 58
17. Plat Map Madison Township, Van Buskirk Farms. 61
18. Family Reunion, mid-1880s 63
19. Fort Wayne College of Medicine, 1900 65
20. Football Team, Fort Wayne College of Medicine, 1902 66
21. Dr. Van Buskirk's reversed painting on glass shingle. 67
22. Van Buskirk home on Maxine Drive, Fort Wayne in 2002. 69
23. Gravestone, Edmund Michael and Mary Louise Van Buskirk. 70

24. Descendants of Edmund Linford and Dorothy E. Van Buskirk. . . . 80
25. Single page from Andrew Van Buskirk's Oregon Trail Journal 94
26. Oregon Trail wagon wheel ruts 99
27. Blue Mountains of Eastern Oregon, 2017. 100
28. Amity Pioneer Cemetery with Van Buskirk Graves 101
29. Genealogical Chart of *The Oregon Trail Van Buskirks* 102
30. Genealogical Chart of Captain David Van Buskirk 108
31. Fenced nineteenth-century grave in Roanoke, Indiana 115
32. Graves of Aaron Elliott Van Buskirk Family 117
33. Genealogical Chart of Aaron Elliott Van Buskirk, MD 118
34. E. Michael Van Buskirk, graduation from medical school 128
35. Family at banquet of the American Glaucoma Society
    that honored E. Michael Van Buskirk, MD, 2006 130
36. Family Photograph, 50th Anniversary 133
37. Descendants of Bette J. and E. Michael Van Buskirk 134

PORTRAITS

1. James Van Buskirk 59
2. George Van Buskirk 59
3. Joseph Van Buskirk, MD 59
4. Linford Van Buskirk 62
5. School picture, Edmund Michael and Otis Walter Van Buskirk. . . . 71
6. Edmund Michael Van Buskirk, high school photograph 71
7. Capt. Edmund Michael Van Buskirk, MD, ca. World War I 72
8. Edmund Michael Van Buskirk, MD, district chairman, Indiana State Medical Society 72
9. Edmund Michael Van Buskirk, MD, president, Indiana State Medical Society 72
10. Edmund Linford Van Buskirk, age 4–5, with mother and sister 78
11. Edmund Linford Van Buskirk, as a young man, late 1920s 78
12. Edmund Linford Van Buskirk, MD, ca. 1960 79
13. Edmund Linford Van Buskirk, MD, ca. 1990s 79
14. William Van Buskirk 103
15. David Van Buskirk 106
16. Aaron Elliott Van Buskirk, MD 111
17. Edmund Michael Van Buskirk, age 3 with father, 1944 123
18. Van Buskirk Family, 1949 at restaurant in Williamsport, Indiana . . 124
19. Edmund Michael Van Buskirk, college graduation 127
20. Edmund Michael Van Buskirk, MD, 2003 132
21. Edmund Michael Van Buskirk, MD, 2014 132

PREFACE

On a crisp November day in 1994, my wife Bette, daughter Sarah, and I visited my eighty-seven-year-old father at his new house in Lafayette, Indiana. Our specific purpose was for Sarah and me to gather as much information as possible from him about the notorious body-snatching exploits of one of our distant, but intriguing, cousins.

Aaron Elliott Van Buskirk, MD, had been a professor of surgical anatomy at the Medical College of Fort Wayne, Indiana in the late 1800s. The story had already been filtered through at least three generations, told and retold in wildly variable iterations and embellishments. Over a century later, in preparation for a book on the subject, we were embarking on an attempt to sift the facts from the fables. As my dad reminisced at length with stories he recalled from his own life, every so often he would leave his chair, go to the basement, and return with a folder containing documentation with some tidbit about those events and many others. We learned that Aaron Elliott (often called "A.E.") Van Buskirk was from a different branch of the family, the nephew to my great-great-grandfather James, but he had taught my grandfather at the medical college in Fort Wayne and had been an intimate contributor to our family lore.

As the day with my father wore on, our notebooks were but half full, but it soon became time for us to leave if we were to catch our scheduled flight. We said our good-byes—not easy to do with an elderly parent who lived three time zones away. We got ourselves settled in the rental car and were just pulling into the street when he called from the doorstep for us to wait. He disappeared into the house, and then came out to the car carrying a bulky packing case that was brimming with musty old documents like those he had shown us earlier.

"Here," he said, "I want you to take this."

I told him I couldn't. I wasn't comfortable taking his precious treasure; I said I would get them next time.

But he insisted I take them "now."

My wife, Bette, urged me with a gentle poke to the ribs to take them, then and there, so I did. (I never saw my father again: he died a few months later.)

When I finally had a chance to examine the box's contents at home, I found many old documents of our family history, collected by my grandfather, even my great-grandfather. Among the items were my father's long correspondence with Irene Shoemaker, the genealogical author of *Van Buskirk, A Legacy from New Amsterdam*[5], a reversed photostat of Laurens Andriessen's original will in the old Dutch language, and my grandfather's English translation of the will meticulously typed onion skin paper. As my family has migrated from place to place, East Coast to West, much more comfortably than the ancestors I describe, I have carried these documents as a sort of collective familial amulet. I have always known where they were, because I knew that, someday, I would want and need to make sense of it all. This is my attempt to do so.

On these pages, I have recounted the story of the Van Buskirk emigration to North America in the mid-1650s and of the family's progressive westward migrations across North America that continued for the subsequent ten generations. I focus upon those people directly in the genealogical line of descent for my particular branch of the family, but I also include a few of the varied tales about some of the more distant Van Buskirk cousins. I have designated our branch of eleven generations the "Fort Wayne Van Buskirks," because it was in that community in Allen County, Indiana, where James Van Buskirk, my great-great-grandfather settled to farm in the mid-nineteenth-century, to be followed by his son Linford. In turn, my grandfather and namesake Edmund Michael Van Buskirk became a prominent physician in Fort Wayne in the first half of the twentieth century, followed by my father, Edmund Linford Van Buskirk who became an equally renowned physician some hundred miles to the west in Lafayette, Indiana. In addition, not in our direct line was the family of James's younger brother, Jacob, whose two sons and two daughters settled in Fort Wayne but by way of a far more circuitous route, as discussed in a separate chapter.

I have gleaned information from a wide variety of sources including documents collected by my grandfather and father in the first half of the twentieth century. I have also relied upon books from the nineteenth and twentieth centuries, and some original sources from Fort Wayne such as wills, deeds, court reports, death certificates, and newspaper articles. Recently, I have perused additional copious material (undocumented) from the internet, genealogical and a variety of historical websites, as well as some original internet articles. These have provided a multitude of data, but always need to be confirmed from a verifiable source. I am neither a historian nor a genealogist, but I have relied on historical—and what I believe to be reliable—genealogical sources. I have made every effort to verify events and dates, and I have endeavored to indicate in the text where controversy or uncertainty may exist.

For accurate genealogical information, I have leaned most heavily upon Irene Shoemaker's monumental two-volume book, *Van Buskirk, A Legacy from New Amsterdam*, published in 1990.[S] Her statements are invariably supported with reference to source documents. When I find disagreement, I have generally used her data, but recognize that the work is not entirely free from error in the light of our perspective from the several decades that have passed since her publication. In addition, the wonderful series of four articles in the *Proceedings of the New Jersey Historical Society, Third Series, 1906–1907* by William Nelson entitled "The Founder of the Van Buskirk Family in America,"[N] has provided additional reliable information and has amplified my understanding and "feel" for the times. Richard Shorto's *The Island at the Center of the World*[Sh] provides many of the details of Dutch New Netherlands historical background.

On the practical side, I have employed three kinds of annotations to document the story. I have included a bibliography of general references, mainly books, a few articles, and websites that I have listed alphabetically at the end. Because I have used numerical superscripts to indicate the generation to which a specific individual belongs, I have used alphabetical superscripts for bibliographic references, using the first letters of the author's surname.

An additional word on genealogical superscript may also be needed. In the individual chapter introductions, I have assigned each direct ancestor a numerical superscript to indicate the particular generation in North America to which that person belongs. I have started with Laurens^1 Andriessen Van Buskirk as the first generation Van Buskirk, followed by his son, Andries^2, and so on down the genealogical path to my father as Edmund^{10} Linford and to myself, Edmund^{11} Michael. This becomes especially important when individuals with the same given names but of different generations co-exist. For example George^4 Van Buskirk's son Joseph^5 Van Buskirk and his son, Joseph^6 Van Buskirk, both lived well into the 1800s. It becomes even more crucial when, for example, one confronts situations whereby George's^4 older son John^5 (Joseph's^5 older brother) also had a son name Joseph, designated Joseph^{6b}, who was born just a few years before our Joseph^6. I have thus reserved the use of numerical superscripts to indicate the generation to which an individual belongs, not as bibliographic endnotes for which I have used alphabetical characters. At the same time, considering that the Van Buskirks in America began with one man, Laurens^1 Andriessen Van Buskirk, likely arriving around 1654, I have designated his generation as number 1, his children as number 2 and so on. Actually, Laurens^1 Andriessen Van Buskirk, relative to other early settlers, was a latecomer to New Amsterdam in 1654, so it should not be surprising that his sons married into families who had preceded him in North America. Thus, those of us who descend from Jan^3 (John^3) Van Buskirk can also trace our descent through his wife, Marytie Hoochlandt, to Joris and Catalina Trico

De Rapelje of the generation preceding Laurens[1] Andriessen, and who were among the very first group of settlers at Fort Orange in 1625.

I have described the first two generations of Van Buskirks in North America in some detail to include the arrival of Laurens[1] Andriessen Van Buskirk and the dispersion throughout the New Netherlands colony of his four sons, Andries[2], Laurens[2], Pieter[2], and Thomas[2]. Naturally, the records of the four sons are the most sparse and scattered of our ancestors, and yet are crucial to the understanding of our deepest roots. Much of what we can know about their lives comes from the legal records that have remained—their births, marriages, and deaths—but also from their official appointments, appearances in court, and especially their purchase and sale of property. Fortunately for us who are now curious about their lives three centuries ago, these early settlers were nothing if not voracious land speculators. They bought, held, and sold what today would be huge tracts of land in the New York, New Jersey, and Hudson Valley regions. If I have provided a bit more detail about the eldest son, Andries[2], it is because it is through him that we trace our descent from his father, Laurens[1] Andriessen Van Buskirk. Through Andries's[2] son, John[3] Van Buskirk, we can trace the circuitous migration of our ancestors through Pennsylvania, Ohio, and Indiana in the aftermath of the Revolutionary War. Thus, with some notable exceptions, beyond the first two generations, I confine further discussion to the fourth son of Andries[2] Van Buskirk, John[3] (Jan or Johannes), and his direct descendants. However, I have also included some anecdotes about some of our more fascinating distant cousins in the chapters entitled "Byways of the Distant Cousins." Here, I have added an additional annotation to the generational superscript number, designating the descendants of Laurens[1] Van Buskirk and xxxxxx[3L] or xxxxxx[4L] and so on. In the discussion of the two Josephs[6], I have added a "b" to the superscript, as in Joseph[6b], to distinguish him from Joseph[6], our direct ancestor. By the same token, I have designated the cousins on the Oregon Trail as xxxxxx[6ot] or xxxxxx[7ot] and the ancestors of David Van Buskirk as xxxxxx[4d], et cetera.

ORIGINS OF THE VAN BUSKIRK NAME

Anyone named "Van Buskirk" will eventually be queried about the origin of his or her surname, neither rare nor pedestrian, but commonly encountered and often misconstrued. Of the many possible mispronunciations, most common, in my own experience, is "Van Burskirk," "Van Bursick," or "Buzzkirk," but many variations in preference, spelling, and pronunciation exist. Even among the Van Buskirk descendants, the name has changed and continues to change over the 350-odd years of its existence in North America, from "Buskirk" to "Boskirk," "Van Berskerk," "Van Booskirk," "Buskirk," "Van Boskerck," and many more. Moreover, the two words separated by a space befuddles many a computer database leading to either "VanBuskirk" or "Buskirk," thus pervading the genealogy of the millennial generation. Annoying as this may be to the purists among us, it may be of some consolation to acknowledge that not only has the name and spelling evolved widely since the original New Amsterdam settlers of the seventeenth century, but it was, in fact, a "made up name."

BACKGROUND

After Henry Hudson's discovery of what he believed to be a probable northwest sea passage to the "Indies," the Dutch foresaw a great urgency for them to establish Dutch settlements in the new lands in order to gain ascendancy over the British claims to the North American Hudson Valley. After the successful model of the Dutch East India Company, then dominating spice trade from the east, they rapidly formed a Dutch West India Company to develop trade in North America, especially for the abundance of timber, and for the fur that Henry Hudson had described.

Anxious to recruit any able-bodied folk who were ready to make the arduous sea journey, the Dutch West India Company offered substantial plots of land in the New World in exchange for six years service to the "company." Among the first of those interested was a group of Walloon refugees who were newly arrived from the Flemish Lowlands after having fled the violence of the French Reformation. Included with these Walloons was a young unmarried couple, Joris De Rapelje and his Parisian fiancé, Catalina Trico. Although Joris De Rapelje was an illiterate Walloon textile worker from the lowlands, his family traced their noble origins to eleventh-century Bretagne, France.[Sh,Mi] His grandfather Colonel Gaspard Colet de Rapelje had lost his title, land, and fortune to the French Catholic insurgence and had barely escaped the massacre of some two hundred Protestant noblemen on the eve of St Bartholomew's

Day, August 24, 1572 (aka St. Bartholomew's Day massacre). The subsequently impoverished Rapeljes had fled first to Switzerland and eventually settled among the Walloons in the Dutch Lowlands. There, Joris de Rapelje met the young Parisian girl named Catalina Trico before they traveled to Amsterdam. As a condition under which the betrothed young couple agreed to undertake the dangerous and arduous emigration to the North American wilderness, the Dutch West India Company consented to arrange for Joris de Rapelje and Catalina Trico to be married. Just four days later, they departed for the three-month voyage on the ship Unity in 1625. Not long after arriving in the new land, Catalina gave birth to the couple's daughter, Sarah, who became the first European child born in the colony of New Netherlands.

The West India Company believed it would be necessary to establish land settlements as a basis for future property claims and commercial ventures. Henry Hudson had described three rivers in the region of what is now New York Bay: The South River (the Delaware), the North River (The Hudson), and the Fresh River (The Connecticut) (see fig. 1). To establish the Dutch claims to the region, the company had stipulated that small conclaves of these early settlers should be settled along each of the three rivers. As the crew of the Unity soon learned, these three rivers were much further apart, by hundreds of miles, than they had been led to believe.[Sh]

Nonetheless, they left a few settlers along the South River (The Delaware) and the Fresh River (The Connecticut) to the east. Desirous of a presence at the mouth of the Hudson, the crew left an even smaller group on Nut Island, a stone's throw from Manhattan Island, before they sailed north, upstream along the Hudson River to its junction with the Mohawk River. There, they established their major encampment, the outpost of Fort Orange, near the site of the future Albany. It seemed a natural location for their settlement because it provided river access to the western interior of North America and was an established place where the interior Indians came to trade. Unfortunately, it also occupied a former hunting ground of the Algonquin-speaking Mahican

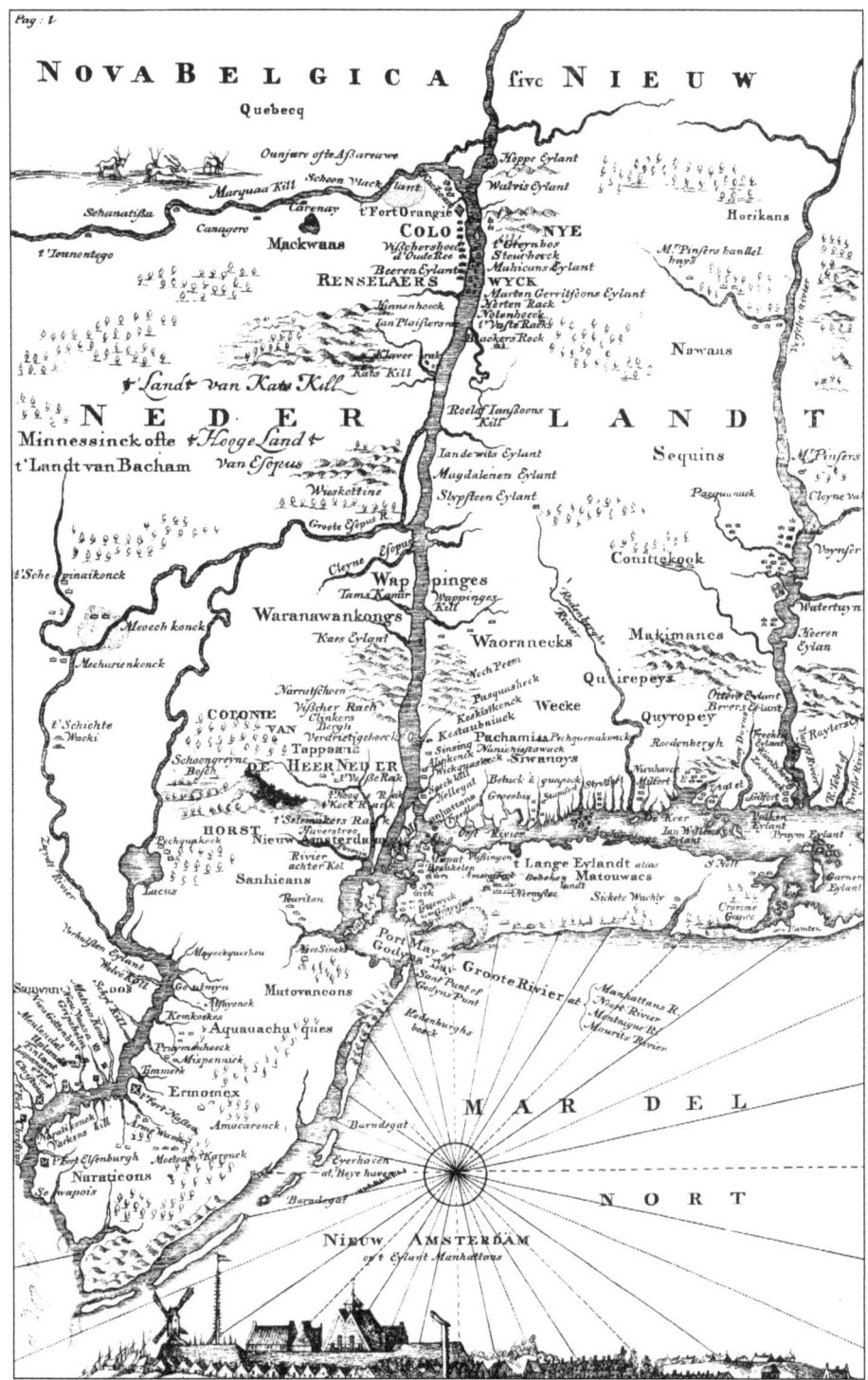

Figure 1. Hudson's Three Rivers: at left, The South (Delaware) River; middle, The North (Hudson) River; at right, The Fresh (Connecticut) River. As shown on Adriaen Van der Donck's 1653 Map of New Netherlands.[V]

Indians and for their traditional rivals, the Mohawk Indians, who were members of the Iroquois League that occupied the lands just to the north. Soon, it also became a site of confrontation between the two factions.

Against West India Company's Indian neutrality policy, the settlers formed a close alliance with the Mahicans. The Fort commander, Daniel van Crieckenbeeck, agreed to side with them in battle against the Mohawks. In short order, van Crieckenbeeck, three other colonists, and twenty-four Mahicans were killed by Mohawk arrows, thus depriving the diminutive Dutch colony of its leader and sending the survivors into anarchic disarray.[Sh]

But Fort Orange was not alone in its administrative dysfunction: each of the new colonial settlements had it own issues and disappointments. The South River bore no resemblance to its reputed Florida-like climate, but was a shallow, marshy, and pestilent swampland that was nearly unlivable. It would not be permanently settled for another forty years. Meanwhile, on Nut Island (now Governor's Island) at the mouth of the North (or Hudson) River, the colonists grew so disgruntled with their Provisional Director, Willem Verhuls, that they banished him and sent him packing back to Holland.

At this point, the overseeing Dutch West India Company decided to abandon their strategy of widely spread small colonies on separate sites. Rather, they would consolidate into a single colony of New Amsterdam that would be accessible by sea and relatively easy to defend. A new leader, Peter Minuet, stepped into the fold with his infamous purchase of Manhattan Island, a stone's throw from Nut Island, as the most suitable location for a permanent settlement. It had a natural and defensible harbor and adequate land for property and fortification, as well as for agriculture and hunting. Within two years, many of the original colonialists at Fort Orange were moved downstream to Manhattan Island. Among these first settlers were Joris and Catalina Rapelje with their new baby, Sarah. They ultimately had a total of eleven children, the fifth of whom was Elisabett Rapelje whose granddaughter married Laurens[1] Andriessen's grandson Jan[3] from whom the Van Buskirks of Fort Wayne are descended.

Background

Although the Van Buskirks descend from the earliest settlers of the Dutch colony of New Netherlands, their patriarch, Laurens[1] Andriessen Van Buskirk, was Scandinavian, born in the Holstein region near the base of the Jutland Peninsula, then of Denmark, now part of Germany. There appears to be little dispute that Laurens[1] Andriessen was born in Holstein around 1625, but documentation of the barest rudiments of his early life have yet to be discovered. Thus, one can only speculate about possible reasons for his emigration to Amsterdam, but they were likely due to some or all of the elements of religion, war, and economic hardship. A terrible tidal storm on the Jutland Peninsula had destroyed homes and property in 1634; the Thirty Years' War raged until 1648; and the fervent vagaries of the ongoing Protestant Reformation drove many from their homelands. Regardless of Laurens's[1] reasons for leaving, Amsterdam was a logical choice: the city had become the melting pot of Europe, welcoming opportunists and refugees of all sorts so long as they were law-abiding and willing to work hard. It had become a popular first stop before contemplating a far more adventuresome migration across the Atlantic (see fig. 2).

CHAPTER 1

THE FIRST GENERATION: VAN BUSKIRKS IN NORTH AMERICA

Laurens Andriessen Van Buskirk (ca. 1625–1694)

Laurens[1] Andriessen Van Buskirk turned wood, making bowls, shoes, and various household goods. He must have arrived in Amsterdam for some extended period of time before he embarked for North America because his woodworking business was well established there. He had acquired an apprentice who travelled with him to the New World.

Laurens[1] Andriessen landed at New Amsterdam on the Isle of Manhattan from Holstein, Denmark, via the Netherlands by 1654. The record is not entirely clear about the exact date of his arrival but offers reasonable suggestions that it was as early as 1652. Many genealogy websites place him first in New Netherlands in 1656, but he had been there at least long enough to witness a baptism in New Amsterdam on December 25, 1654. That was where he followed local custom of adding a Dutch name, "Van Buskirk" (Van Boeskerk-sp) (vonBuschkirk), to his Scandinavian name, indicating from where he had come or where he was situated: Van Buskirk expressing from the "Church in the Wood."

The choice of surname, "from the wood" is of special interest because his homeland Holstein in Old Saxon means "Land of the Wood." By the same token, his fellow countryman and his wife's first husband, Christian Barentsen,

Figure 2. Map of North Central Europe about 1648 (near the time of Laurens Andriessen's migration to Amsterdam), which shows the geographic relationship of Holstein to Amsterdam at that time. Reproduced and adapted from Shepherd's Historical Atlas.[Sp]

had added "Van Hoorn" to indicate that he'd come to the New World from the Dutch city of Hooren. In many of the early documents, Laurens[1] Andriessen Van Buskirk is referred to simply as "De Draijer," the Turner, and sometimes as Laurens De Draijer or Laurens Andriessen de Drayer. Some confusion exists regarding the name Draijer (sometimes spelled Drayer or even Droyer), because it is not a Dutch name for either a woodworker or a maker of wooden household items. However, Nelson explains it best as the Dutch word for turner (wood turner) or drawer, worker with a draw knife.[N] (The contemporary Dutch word for "turner" is "draaier.") In one later deed, he is referenced as "Laurens the Drawer." A prominent point of land still extends well into Newark Bay from his old property on "Bergen Neck" and is known to this day as "Droyer's Point."

The First Generation: Van Buskirks in North America

Laurens[1] Andriessen made wooden housewares for his neighbors and fellow citizens in the village of New Amsterdam. He must have also undertaken a bit of general carpentry as the demand required, for he did work on the fortification wall between the colonial village and the northern reaches of Manhattan Island, the wall that gave its name to that most famous address of the American financial world. Laurens[1] Andriessen's business in Holland had been sufficiently successful to acquire an apprentice, one Fredrick Arentszen, who traveled with him to the New World. After a year or so, the man left to marry a local woman, and Laurens[1] sued him for breaking away from his obligation. At his subsequent marriage, Fredrick Arentszen, like his master, also added a Dutch surname, in his case, Van Swartensluys.[N] By 1656, Laurens[1] had acquired property in the colonial village on both sides of Broad Street where it abutted the fortification wall, which extended from the Hudson to the East River as a protection against potential invasion from the north.

At the Old Dutch Church, Staten Island, on December 12, 1658, Laurens[1] Andriessen Van Buskirk married a young widow named Jannetje Jans. Her first husband, Christian Barentsen Van Hoorn, had, as mentioned earlier, come to New Amsterdam from Hooren, a small city north of Amsterdam. He was also a carpenter, had worked on the fortification wall, and owned property at Broad and Wall Street. Barentsen had been among Peter Stuyvesant's forces that declared victory over the New Sweden colony along the South (Delaware) River on September 5, 1655.[D, Wns]

In a Dutch effort to maintain a viable foothold along the river, the Dutch West India Company allowed the Swedes and Finns to remain and to continue as a semi-independent "Swedish Nation." At the same time, they encouraged Dutch settlement of the old Swedish Fort Trinity that they renamed New Amstel. Christian Barentsen volunteered to help. He returned to the area but became ill and succumbed to an epidemic arising in the marshy lowlands there. Laurens[1] Andriessen may also have gone there to help with the construction, but he escaped the pestilence.

After 1664, the British ultimately were successful at developing the New Amstel colony on the South River as the colony of "New Castle." It survives today as the charming, historic city of New Castle, Delaware.

When Laurens[1] Andriessen married Barentsen's widow, Jannetje Jans, he adopted her three sons. The couple then had four sons together: Andries[2], Laurens[2], Pieter[2], and Thomas[2]. Laurens[1] and Jannetje remained in Manhattan at least until 1660, but they did not stay permanently. In 1662, Laurens[1] acquired 170 acres of property on the west bank of the Hudson River, just across New York Bay from Manhattan at Mingackwa in Bergen County, New Jersey. He and Jannetje moved to the new settlement. (Mingackwa is an Indian word meaning "place of best crossing," and is spelled a variety of ways in the old literature and documents. It lay in one of the narrowest places of Bergen Neck and was the best place to portage from New York Bay to Newark Bay.) Laurens[1] Andriessen Van Buskirk originally purchased his main lot of 170 acres in 1662, and then added 30 additional acres—acquired from his stepson—to thereby extend his land entirely across Bergen Neck (see fig. 3). The English governor, Philip Carteret, officially patented this land to Laurens[1] in 1667. In addition, Laurens's[1] stepson Barents Christian had bought the 30 acres now known as Droyer's Point, and later sold that property to his stepfather. Mingackwa eventually became the community of Greenville, part of the future Jersey City, adjacent to Paulus Hook, a small peninsula that projects into New York Bay. This property remained in the Van Buskirk family for several generations and is what Laurens and Jannetje's will refers to as "The Mingackwa Farm."

The property extended entirely across the narrow land mass of the neck of Constable Hook (now Bergen Neck), from the prominent point (now Droyer's Point) on Newark Bay, just below the mouths of the Hackensack and Passaic Rivers to Paulus Hook, on the west shore of the Hudson River. The tract had originally been allotted to Claas Carstensen (The Norman) as a patent issued by the Dutch Colonial Director General, William Kieft, on March 23, 1647 and designated as Mingackwa Lot #19, as marked on the map[N] (see fig. 3).

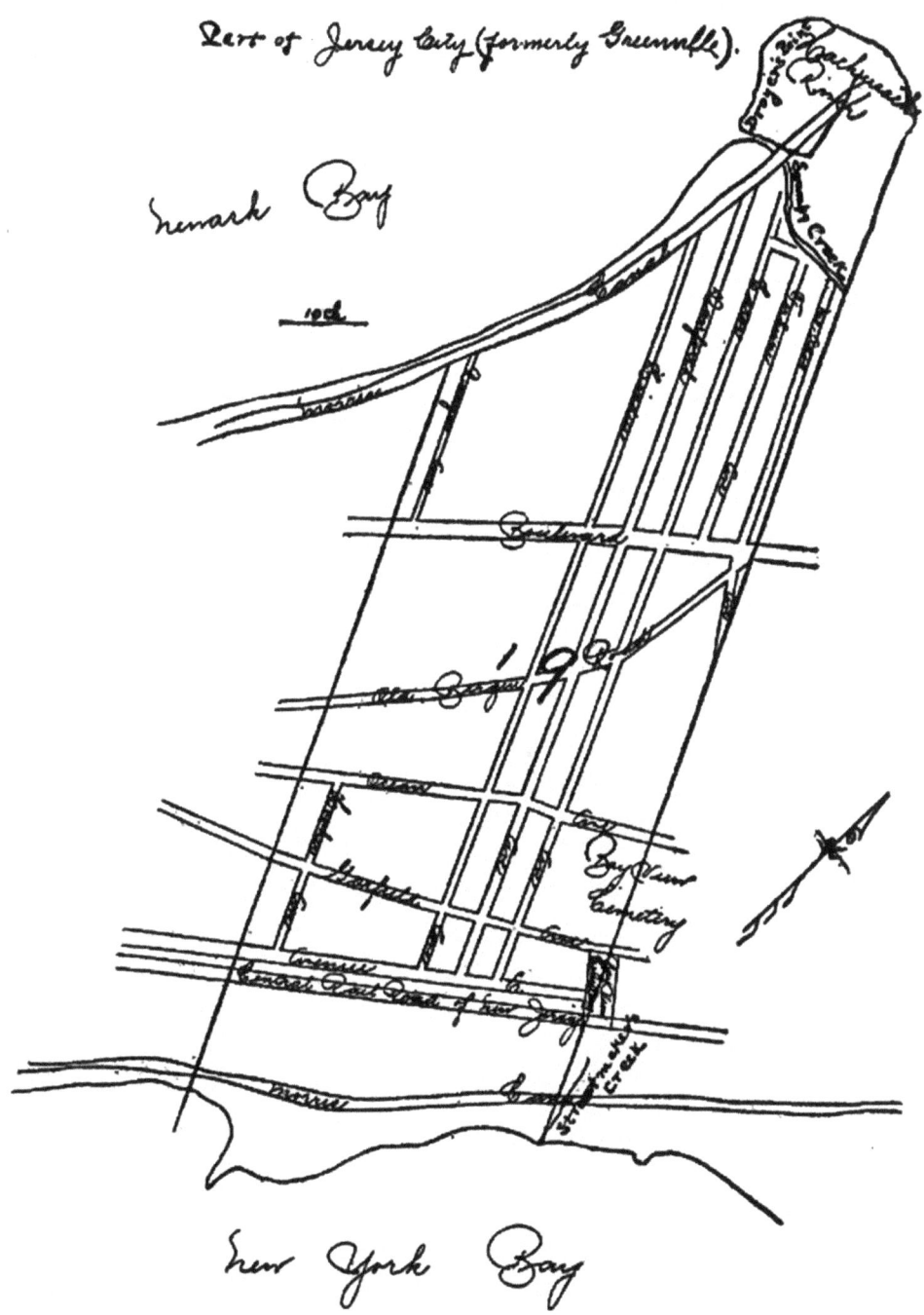

Figure 3. Laurens[1] Andriessen Van Buskirk's Mingackwa Lot 19 superimposed over the 1872 Map of Bergen Neck, Greenville, NJ. Lot 19 extended from Paulus Hook on New York Bay at bottom and Droyer's Point on Newark Bay, at top. Lot 19 Overlay from Nelson[N], originally from Winfield.[W2]

The point extending into Newark Bay became known first as "Draijer's Point," ultimately "Droyer's Point" on maps of 1764.

Laurens[1] soon rose to leadership in the colonial village, serving on the colonial councils and as advisor to the governor. Although he continued to work as a wood turner much of his life, like many of his fellow settlers, much of his family wealth derived from what now would be considered land speculation. In May of 1668, Laurens[1] acquired two additional lots in Bergen, of 18 acres and 12 acres respectively, but sold those some time later. After the British took New Amsterdam from the Dutch in 1664, he declared his allegiance to the English governor and successfully petitioned to retain both his land and his political appointments. He did the same when the Dutch retook the colony in 1673 and repeated the process when the British recaptured it for good in 1674.

As a member of the Governor's council, Laurens[1] had overseen the purchase on behalf of the French Huguenots, known as the French Company, of several square miles of Bergen County land that extended easterly from the Hackensack River to the Palisades, along Hudson River. This land lay adjacent to a similar tract of land that Laurens[1] had purchased from Indians sometime before. However, he had no documented patent on this land until 1682 when it was executed, on behalf of Governor Philip Carteret by Lady Elizabeth Carteret, "in favor of Mr. Laurence Anderson of 'Bergen' for a track of land 1076 acres," extending easterly from Hackensack River to Englewood (see figs. 4 and 5).

Both Laurens[1] and his wife became ill in 1679 and prepared their final will. However, they both recovered and lived until the last decade of the seventeenth century. Jannetje died on March 16, 1692, and Laurens[1], two years later, on July 13, 1694. Their will provided the following:

- Survivor spouse to retain entire estate to her/his death.
- Each child, including three by previous marriage, to receive 400 guilders to be paid in "seewant" (Indian Shell Money).

The First Generation: Van Buskirks in North America

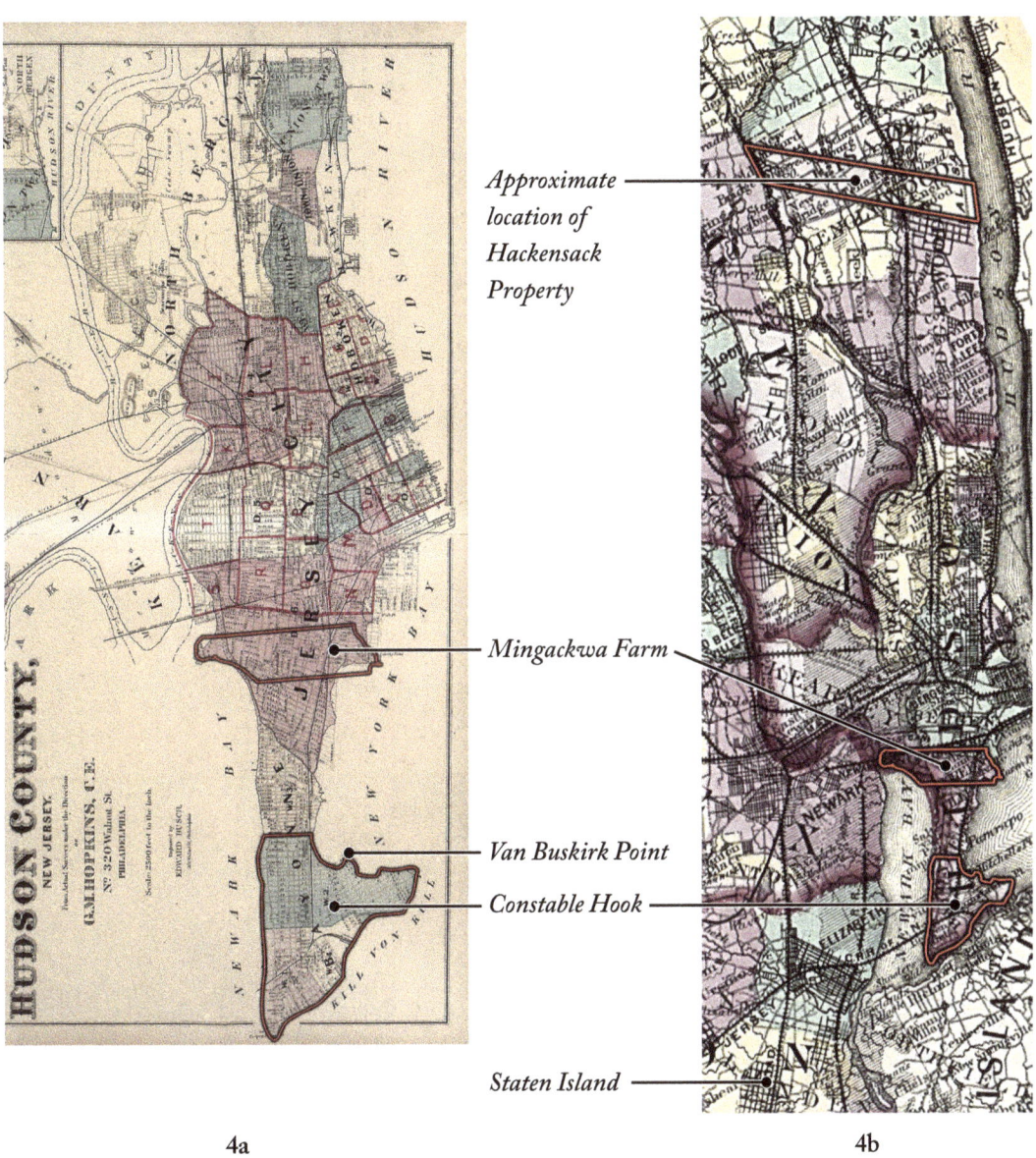

Figure 4. Laurens¹ Andriessen Van Buskirk's Properties at the time of his death in 1694. The more exploded view, 4a, shows the Bergen Neck with the Mingackwa Farm overlain from Paulus Hook to Droyer's Point; it also shows Constable Hook (later owned by Pieter Van Buskirk) in some detail. View 4b shows western Bergen County (and Hudson Co.) in less detail but with the Hackensack Property in Northern Bergen County. Map source: Hopkins, G. M. & G.M. Hopkins & Co. (1873), combined atlas of the state of New Jersey and the late township of Greenville, now part of Jersey City, from actual survey official records and private plans.[Ho]

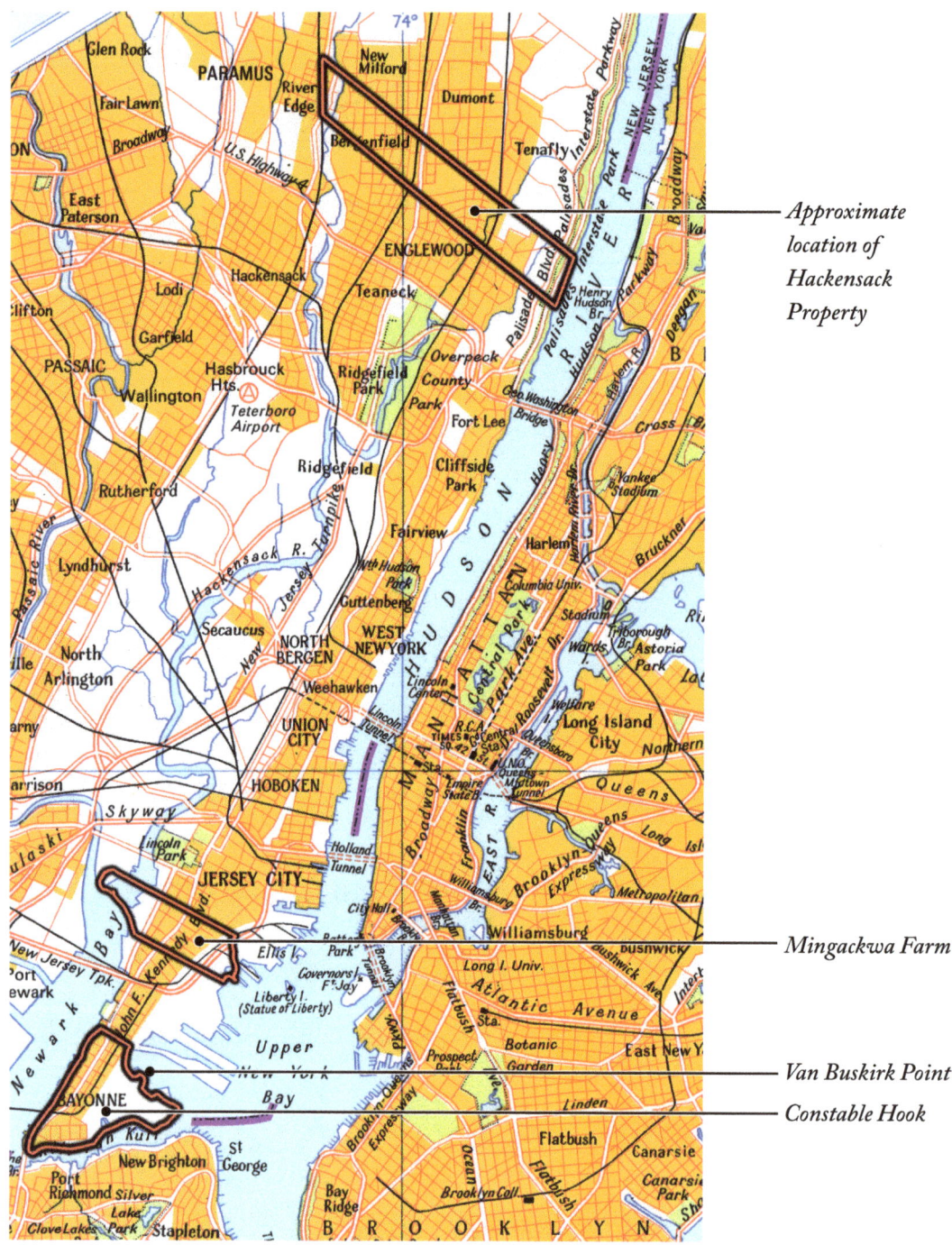

Figure 5. Van Buskirk Bergen County Property at time of Laurens¹ Andriessen Van Buskirk's death is superimposed on this contemporary map of New York (see fig. 4 for comparison.) Black dots on Mingackwa Farm represent Droyer's Point on left and Paulus Hook on the right. Map Source: The Times Atlas of the World, Eighth Comprehensive Edition, New York and Environs.[Ta]

- Thomas and Pieter receive the Minchackque Farm as their portion of the estate.
- Each son to receive a 70 rod-wide (385 yards) lot at Hackensack.
- Remainder of estate, (mainly property at Hackensack of 1056 acres) to be divided in half, the first half, to the seven sons of Jannetje (i.e., three by her first husband and four with Laurens[1]), and the second half among the four sons of Laurens[1] Andriessen Van Buskirk. Thus the sons of Laurens[1] were to receive 7.14 percent from their mother and 12.5 percent from their father or 20 percent each. The three sons of the mother by first husband were to receive 7.14 percent each.
- Remainder of estate to remain with survivor.

By the time of his death, Laurens[1], owned the Minchackque (Mingackwa) Farm that cut completely across the Bergen Neck from Paulus Point on the Hudson side (Bay of New York) to Droyer's Point on the Bay of Newark. In addition, he owned the huge tract at New Hackensack that extended from Englewood on the Hudson shore to the Hackensack River.

CHAPTER 2

SECOND GENERATION: FOUR SONS OF LAURENS ANDRIESSEN VAN BUSKIRK

Andries, Laurens, Pieter, and Thomas.

After their parents' deaths, the two older sons, Andries[2] and Laurens[2], retained the property in Hackensack, and the two younger sons, Pieter[2] and Thomas[2], the Mingackwa Farm. Andries[2] also owned 26 acres of meadow between Mingackwa and Constable Hook, presumably part of his father's estate. In 1698, he exchanged this property with his half brother for 30 acres "on the north side of the Kill van Kull" that would have been the southern shore of Constable Hook. Kill van Kull is the shipping channel between Newark Bay to the east and New York Bay on the west, and between Staten Island on the south and Constable Hook to the north (see fig. 5). This must have been a land investment because, according to Winfield[W2], Andries[2] resided with his brother Laurens[2] at Saddle River.[W] On May 1, 1701, Andries[2] bought, with nine other men, the so-called "Horseneck Tract" of land, east of the Passaic River to the hills, a tract of 14,000 acres in what is now Essex County, New Jersey. On Oct 14, 1723, Andries[2] sold to his brother Laurens[2] his interest in his father's farm for £1200. Actually, Irene Shoemaker states that he released his "interest in his father's land," suggesting that it was all of the property he had inherited from his father, not just the farm.[S]

Andries[2] married Jannetje Van der Linde, the daughter of Joost Van der Linde and Fytje Van Gelder. They had four sons: Laurens[3], Andries[3], Joost[3], and Johannes (John)[3]; and three daughters: Fytje[3], Anna[3], and Helena[3]. The second son, Andries[3], appears to have died young, for his name is no longer mentioned in the family records or listed in his father's will. After Jannetje died in 1716, Andries[2] married Anna Grevenraedt on April 2, 1720. Andries[2] died April 1, 1732 and was buried April 3, 1732 at the Constable Hook family cemetery. In his will, proved April 17, 1732, Andries[2] left to his second wife, Anna Grevenraedt, some personal possessions and the right to live in house for one year. In addition, she was to receive from his son Lawrence (English version of "Laurens") the rents of two of his houses on Pearl Street as well as the rents of the "least of his houses" on John Street, in Manhattan. After his wife's death, his daughter Fytje[3] was to receive these rents from the John Street property. In the will, Andries[2] points out that in his lifetime he has already taken care of all of his children by distributing his real estate among them. Half of his residual estate was left to his wife and, in turn, on her death, to his three daughters. The other half went to Laurens[3], his eldest son. The two younger sons, Joost[3] and John[3], had already received, long before, substantial property in Pennsylvania and were living at the Manor of Moreland as described with the third generation.

If only because they and their offspring tended to stay put, the best known of Laurens[1] Andriessen Van Buskirk's four sons are actually the three youngest because their names and even their houses have lasted into the parlance of the contemporary era. Pieter's[2] house on Van Buskirk Point of Constable Hook stood until the late 1890s when it was torn down as part of the Standard Oil purchase. His brother Thomas[2] Van Buskirk's house at Saddle River still stands today on the National Registry of Historic Homes. In addition, one finds Van Buskirk Point, Van Buskirk Island, and numerous other Van Buskirk monikers throughout the contemporary state of New Jersey.

Baptismal records have not been located for Laurens[2] Van Buskirk, the second son of Laurens[1] Andriessen Van Buskirk, but he was born between 1660 and 1666. Laurens[1] Andriessen and Jannetje Van Buskirk, had, by that time, moved from New Amsterdam, across New York Bay, to the Mingackwa farm in Bergen. Laurens[2] married Hendrickje Van der Linde, sister of Andries' first wife, Jannetje, both of whom were the daughters of Joost Van der Linde and Fytje Van Gelder. No official record of the marriage has been located but is said by Shoemaker to have taken place in 1691.[S] Laurens[2] and Hendrickje had nine children: seven sons and two daughters.

Laurens[2] is believed to have resided alongside his brother Andries[2] on the Saddle River property. Later, Laurens[2] bought his brother Andries's[2] property share of their father's estate for £1200 on Oct 4, 1723, proved April 7, 1731. In addition, in 1697, Laurens[2] obtained a patent for 240 acres on Hackensack River and Overpeck Creek adjoining lands of his brothers Pieter[2] and Thomas[2] and of his half brother Barent Christian Barentsen. Laurens[2] was elected to the fifth Provincial Assembly of New Jersey, representing Bergen County in 1709.

Laurens[2] lived out his life in the Hackensack region and left his various properties in what is now northeast New Jersey to his children in his will dated May 8, 1722.[N] He died in May of 1724, and the will was proved June 4, 1724. These combined properties were the Hackensack properties originally bought by his father, Laurens[1] Andriessen Van Buskirk, and included Schaalenburg and, a short distance away, the island in the Hackensack River that became Van Buskirk Island (see fig. 5). As described in a later chapter, this region was a Tory stronghold and many, though not all, of Laurens's[2] children became Loyalists during the Revolutionary War and eventually evacuated to eastern Canada.[Sa]

The second generation's third son, Pieter[2] Van Buskirk, 1666–1738, was baptized Jan. 1, 1666 at the Dutch Church, Constable Hook, Bergen County, New Jersey. Pieter[2] married Trientie (Catherine) Harmeanse who was the daughter of Hans Harmeanse and Willemtje Warnaers of Long Island. Willemtje was the widow of Harmen Van Borckeloo. The Harmeanses had

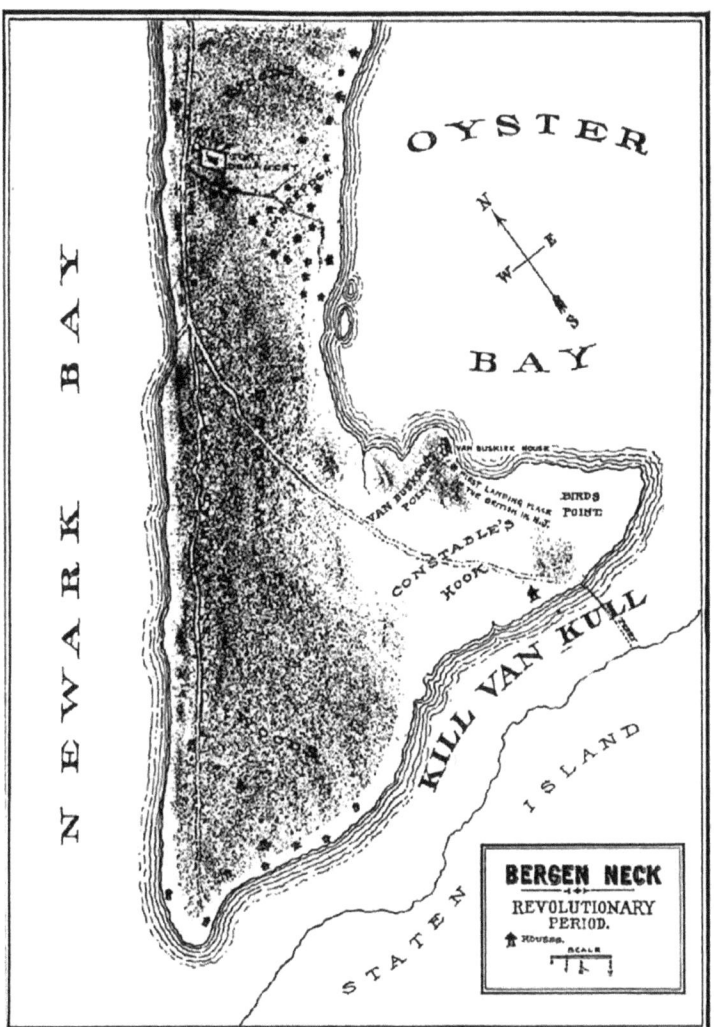

Figure 6. Bergen Neck Map showing Van Buskirk Point and Constable Hook during the Revolutionary War. Pieter Van Buskirk's House is indicated and stood on the point until it was torn down in 1896. Map Source: Pennsylvania Evening Post.[Pe]

moved to Constable Hook, where Hans claimed lands on July 30, 1681 that were granted by deed, Feb. 30, 1695 (bought from Samuel Edsell of Long Island). Pieter[2] Van Buskirk acted as the representative of his wife, Trientie, when her father's estate was partitioned in 1700. Trientie inherited one-half of her father's farm, which comprised the whole of Constable Hook, New Jersey. Trientie's nephew, Hartman Claesen Vreeland, inherited the other half, as the sole heir of his mother (Trientie's sister), Annetje Janse Borckeloo, on Dec. 30, 1730, and he then sold his half to Pieter[2] as well.[N] When these transactions were completed, Pieter[2] Van Buskirk became the sole owner of the whole of Constable Hook, as his father-in-law had been (see figs. 6 and 7). There, Pieter[2] Van Buskirk built their home on the southern slope of Van Buskirk's Point, overlooking New York Bay, the contemporary New York Harbor (see fig. 7). This property sold to Standard Oil at the end of the nineteenth century. The house was torn down, and a large oil refinery was built there that remains today. The Van Buskirk graves were largely destroyed although some were moved to the Moravian Cemetery on Staten Island.

THE VAN BUSKIRK HOMESTEAD, CONSTABLE'S HOOK, ERECTED ABOUT 1690.

Figure 7. Above, drawing of Pieter Van Buskirk House before it was torn down in 1896; below, drawing of Pieter Van Buskirk's gravestone; the original stone was lost after the property was sold to Standard Oil. These drawings were done by I. H. Alexander and published by Winfield in 1874, as reproduced from Nelson.[W,N]

Major Thomas[2] Van Buskirk, 1668–1747, was the youngest son of Laurens[1] Andriessen and Jannetje Jans Van Buskirk. Thomas[2] married Margritie Van der Linde Brickers, but no marriage records have been located. The first of the couple's nine children, Johannis, was baptized on July 1,1694; the ninth, Geertru, was baptized March 7, 1715. Major Thomas[2] married a second time to Volkertie Collier on May 18, 1720 and had seven more children, three boys and four girls. Thomas died in Hunterdon County, New Jersey, and the will was proved on October 20, 1748. An inventory was taken of his belongings on March 1, 1747, suggesting that he had died in February of that year. He is buried in the Schomp Family Burial Ground at Pleasant Run, NJ. A broken headstone that presumably is for him (engraved "TVB") is dated 1747. In the final years of his life, he had moved in with his son in Hunterdon County. The Schomp family were neighbors.

With his brother Pieter[2], Thomas[2] had inherited the farm at Mingackwa from his father, but Thomas[2] sold his share of the land to his older brother Andries[2]. Thomas[2] bought a large tract of land (1090 acres) in the northern part of Bergen County on the Saddle River from John Johnston of New York City by deed of June 3, 1718 for £220.[5] The land had originally been bought from the Indians. Irene Shoemaker states that the house, which eventually became known as the Thomas Van Buskirk House, had been built as a one-room dwelling in 1707, eleven years before Van Buskirk bought it. Further, she asserts that, actually, he likely bought the Saddle River Property from Albert Zabriske in 1708. Although Thomas[2] died in Hunterdon County, New Jersey, he left the Saddle River house to his son Abraham[3]. It remained in the Van Buskirk family for two centuries until it was sold in 1922. It stands today on the National Historic Registry as the Thomas Van Buskirk House at Saddle River, New Jersey (see fig. 8).

Major Thomas[2] had become quite active in Northern New Jersey community life and was prominent in the opening of the Morris County, New Jersey, settlement. He sold 1500 acres in Hunterdon County on both sides of the

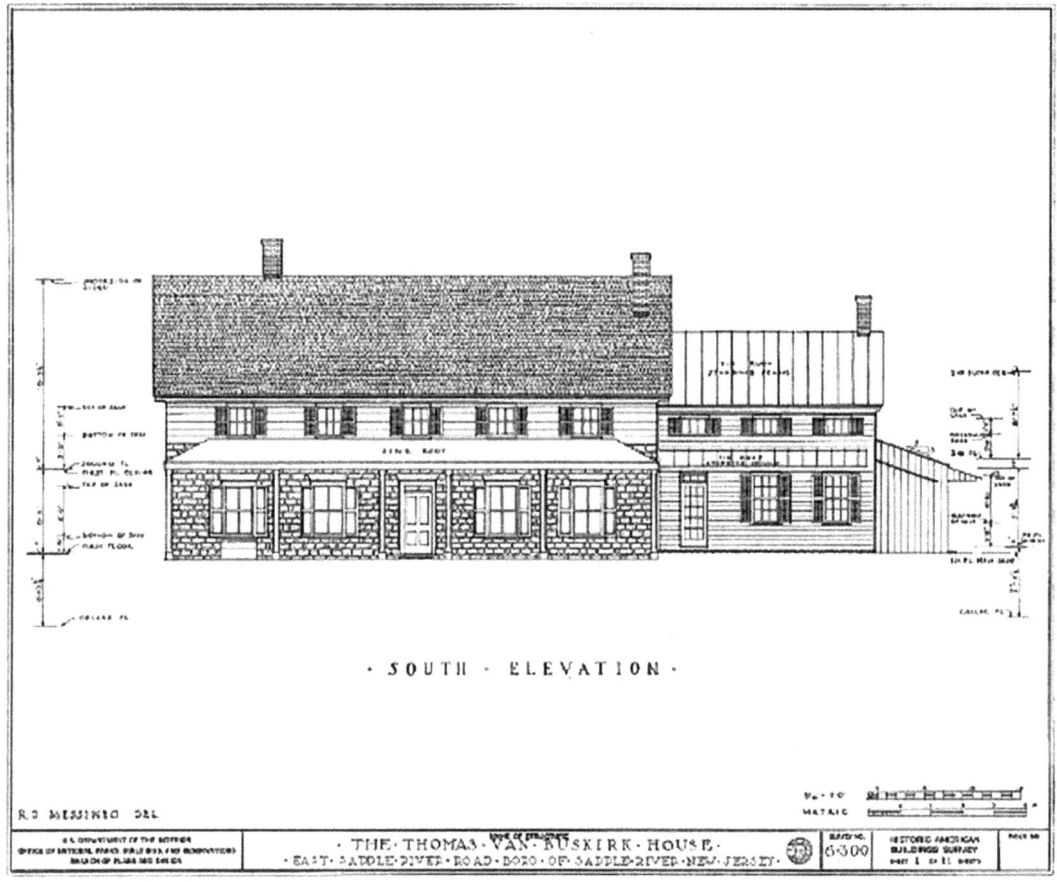

Figure 8. Thomas Van Buskirk House, Saddle River, New Jersey, is on the National Registry of Historic Places at the Library of Congress.[Hi]

Rockaway River—a branch of the "Pesayuck" (Passaic) River, where Montville, New Jersey, is now located. He had also bought land near Readington, in Hunterdon County, near to his son Pieter[3] Van Buskirk who had settled in Lebanon Township, about 20 miles away. In his old age, Major Thomas[2] went there to live; he died at Readington in 1747. Some references claim that he was a Colonel in the British Army during the French and Indian War, but he had died long before that. He left the Saddle River land to his son Abraham and the remainder of the lands in Hunterdon and Sussex Counties to his sons Johannis[3], Isaac[3], Pieter[3], and Michael[3].

In all, by the time of their deaths, the four sons of Laurens[1] Andriessen Van Buskirk held thousands of acres of land in the present state of New Jersey, including on Bergen Neck, most of Constable Hook, and around 2000 acres of what is now Englewood, at the western end of the present-day George Washington Bridge (see fig. 9).

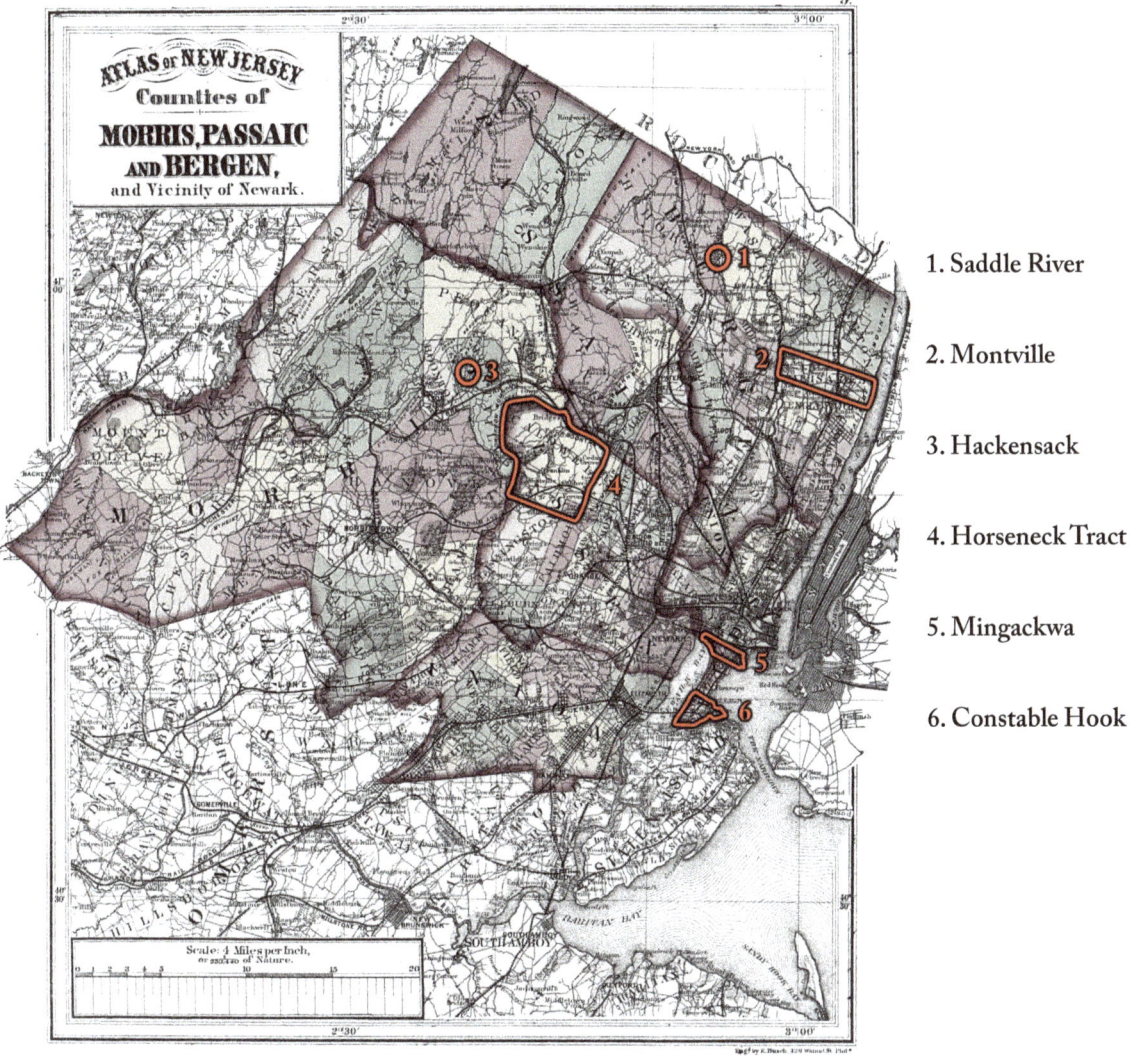

1. Saddle River
2. Montville
3. Hackensack
4. Horseneck Tract
5. Mingackwa
6. Constable Hook

Figure 9. Property of Laurens[1] Andriessen Van Buskirk and his four sons in the seventeenth to eighteenth centuries in Northwest New Jersey. Andries[2] invested with nine other men in the 14,000 acre Horseneck Tract while, with Major Thomas[2], he sold the Montville investment property of 1500 acres, but the remaining properties were held for at least the first two generations. Map Source: Hopkins, G. M. & G.M. Hopkins & Co. (1873), combined atlas of the state of New Jersey and the late township of Greenville, now part of Jersey City, from actual survey official records and private plans.[Ho]

CHAPTER 3

THE THIRD GENERATION: JAN (JOHN) VAN BUSKIRK

(ca. 1670s–1730s)

Our direct Van Buskirk ancestors have descended from Laurens[1] Andriessen Van Buskirk's eldest son, Andries[2] Van Buskirk, through his fourth son, John[3] (Johannes or Jan). John[3] and his brother Joost[3] each received from their father two tracts of land in Pennsylvania: 1150 acres in Buck's County on October 12, 1713; and an adjacent large tract of 186 acres in the Manor of Moreland, Philadelphia County, now Montgomery County, in 1721. Jan or John[3] must have been born in the 1670s, but no birth record for him or his older brother has been located.

John[3] Van Buskirk married Marytie Hoochlandt (Hogeland) at Staten Island on May 5, 1696. Through Marytie Hoochlandt, the descendants of John[3] Van Buskirk trace their ancestry to those original settlers of Fort Orange, New Netherlands. Marytie's paternal grandmother was Elisabett De Rapelje, daughter of Joris and Catalina De Rapelje who had arrived on the ship Unity in the year 1625. As described in the preface, Elisabett's mother, Catalina Trico, married Joris De Rapelje just four days before the Unity sailed from Amsterdam. Elisabett's older sister, Sarah De Rapelje, was the first European woman born in New Netherlands. John[3] and Marytie Hoochlandt Van Buskirk had six children: Jannetje[4], Samuel[4], Andrew[4], George[4], Antje[4], and Daniel[4]. Jannetje[4] was born on December 21, 1714, baptized June 5, 1715, and Samuel[4], baptized June 26, 1716. Both apparently died young and left no further records. Andrew[4] was born 1719, and married Charity Van Horn on July 29, 1742 in Buck's County. Andrew[4] served in the French and Indian War and possibly also in the Revolutionary War. George[4], as detailed in the next chapter, served in the Revolutionary War with his five sons. Antje[4] was baptized on September 30, 1732, and married John Fairweather on August 3, 1761. The sixth child, Daniel[4] Van Buskirk, was born in Buck's County in 1736 but moved to Hunterdon County, New Jersey, where his grandfather Andries[2] Van Buskirk lived out his final days. Daniel[4] ran a public house there.

In 1682, William Penn warranted a 9,815-acre tract of Buck's County land to Dr. Nicholas More, but More died just five years later. The estate sold the properties that were known as "The Manor of Moreland," to various land speculators. In addition to the large plots he had already purchased in Philadelphia County, Andries[2] Van Buskirk bought two adjoining lots of 186 acres, one for each of his sons, John[3] and Joost[3], who moved there between 1714 and 1718. John[3] had married Marytie Hoochlandt before 1716, probably around 1713 or 1714, and Joost[3] married Jemima Wynkoop in 1718. The land was officially conveyed to Joost[3] and John[3] by deed in 1721, but the deed was not recorded until 1755 or 1751 for Joost[3] and never was for John[3]—at least, no records of its recording have survived. Both brothers, however, were living at the Manor of Moreland by 1722. John[3] sold his original property in 1724 and bought a second property also adjacent to his brother Joost[3]. Eventually, John[3] and Marytie bought a tract of property from Jemima (Wynkoop) Van Buskirk's father, Garret Wynkoop, one of the original settlers of The Manor of Moreland. In 1734, John[3] and Marytie Van Buskirk built their house on this land originally bought in 1717 by Garret Wynkoop. The house still stands as part of the Pennypacker Trust, and is known as the Wynkoop House (see fig. 10). John[3] Van Buskirk later sold the property back to the Wynkoops who remained there for several generations.

John³ also had purchased an additional parcel of 200 acres in the north of Buck's county in Northampton Township on Sept 3, 1725, adjacent to a lot of a similar size held by his brother Joost³ (or Joseph) as he was called by that time. John³ sold this lot in January of 1730 and bought yet another lot, that time of 650 acres, also adjacent to his brother's, on August 1, 1730. I believe at least part of this acquisition became the home of his son George⁴ (possibly other children as well) because they are listed as residing in Northampton, Pennsylvania.

Figure 10. Wynkoop House, Upper Moreland, Pennsylvania. Garret Wynkoop purchased the land in the Manor of Moreland around 1717 and apparently sold this lot to John Van Buskirk, Wynkoop's daughter's brother in law. John Van Buskirk built the house in 1734. It has had three additions over the centuries, and is now part of the Pennypacker Ecological Restoration Trust.

CHAPTER 4

THE FOURTH GENERATION: GEORGE VAN BUSKIRK

(1721–1800)

John[3] Van Buskirk's fourth born son, George[4], was baptized on October 8, 1721 at Abington, Pennsylvania and lived in Pennsylvania until his death on March 30, 1800. Some sources other than Shoemaker have recorded his death in 1798, but she seems to have it well documented at the year 1800.[S]

George[4] Van Buskirk married a woman named Sarah, but her surname has not been confirmed. Sarah died between 1774 and 1780. Some genealogists have suggested that George's[4] wife, Sarah, was a Sarah Ashton or Sarah Suzannah Ashton, but no definitive proof has been located. The references arise principally from minutes of Quaker meetings that refer to Sarah Ashton and George Van Buskirk, but do not document that she was George's[4] wife or that she was Sarah Van Buskirk. Thus, they do not constitute definitive proof of their marriage. After Sarah's death, George[4] married for a second time, in 1780, a widow named Anna Weis in Northampton, Pennsylvania, but they had no further children.

George[4] Van Buskirk raised nine children by his first wife, Sarah. He fought in the American Revolutionary War with his five sons (John[5], Lawrence[5], Joseph[5], Andrew[5], and Daniel[5]), as well with his nephew Moses[5], son of his brother Andrew[4]. George's[4] oldest son, John[5], served in the 5th Northampton

Militia Battalion, under Captain Richard Shaw, while George[4], his other four sons, and his nephew Moses Van Buskirk, all served in the 4th Northampton Militia Battalion under Captain John Gregory. After the war, George[4] returned to the family home in Northampton, Pennsylvania, but as often happens in war, his now adult children, veterans of the Revolution, began to scatter. Among the children of George[4] Van Buskirk, the eldest, John[5], moved to Maryland toward the end of the war as indicated by his having witnessed the will of one Jane Linn in Washington County, Maryland in 1783, the final year of the war. Further, the 1790 census shows John[5] living in Maryland, in an area known as the Linten Hundred, Washington County. John's move to Maryland may have been influenced by his captain, Richard Shaw, of the Northampton 5th militia Battalion. There are numerous references to various Shaws in his subsequent official dealings in the Linton Hundred country of Maryland.

George's[4] son Lawrence[5] Van Buskirk and his daughters Sarah[5] (Van Buskirk) Johnson and Susannah[5] (Van Buskirk) Strawn all eventually emigrated west to a Quaker colony in Greene County, at the far southwest corner of Pennsylvania, along the Tenmile Creek. Andrew[5] and the youngest son, Daniel[5], remained in Northampton County, as did Joseph[5] Sr., who returned to run his Northampton inn. His son Joseph[6] Jr., born in 1782, ultimately joined his older relatives in the Tenmile Country in Greene County before moving on to Ohio (see fig. 12).

George[4] Van Buskirk died "intestate" in 1800; the estate was finally settled on October 31, 1801. He had bought from one Phillip Benezet, in 1763, a rather sizable 315-acre tract of farmland in Chestnut Hill Township, Northampton County, Pennsylvania. His son Andrew[5] owned an adjacent plot of 186 acres. According to Pennsylvania law, all of the children were to divide equally their father's 315 acres. However, Sarah[5], Susannah[5], and Lawrence[5] were headed to Greene County, and Andrew[5] owned the farm adjacent to his father's, while Joseph[5] was well ensconced with his inn. Thus, after the estate was settled, all of George's living children agreed to sell their shares to their youngest brother,

The Fourth Generation: George Van Buskirk (1721–1800)

Daniel^5 Van Buskirk, for 550£. By the time George^4 Van Buskirk died, the Van Buskirk western migration was again in full force and merits some further consideration.

CHAPTER 5

THE POST-WAR WESTWARD MIGRATIONS

Each of us North Americans has descended from an immigrant who arrived on this continent from somewhere else. The Van Buskirks are no exception. That arduous journey across the Atlantic Ocean in the middle of the seventeenth century was only the beginning. Each succeeding generation simply had too many surviving offspring for all of them to remain on the family land. Thus, some, often the younger, moved west to more available land, more open spaces. In our case, it was the eldest son of Laurens[1] Andriessen Van Buskirk, Andries[2] Van Buskirk, who bought some 200 acres of Pennsylvania land for his third and fourth sons. Thus, our third generation progenitor, John[3] (Jan) Van Buskirk had settled in the Manor of Moreland in Buck's County by 1722.

Within a few decades, the lure of the west with its new land and new opportunities would increasingly draw subsequent generations, especially in the context of the colonial social and political upheaval in the later part of the eighteenth century. As Howard Lackey points out in his fine description of the pioneer settlement of the Southwestern Pennsylvanian Tenmile Country, it seemed that each generation would push a bit farther west.[L] In his example, the first generation might settle in eastern Pennsylvania, but the subsequent generation would migrate on to the Shenandoah Valley, then the next, a bit further to Tenmile in the southwest corner of Pennsylvania.[L]

So it was with the Van Buskirks. John's[3] son George[4] stayed put, having fought for the patriots in the Revolutionary War, but many of his children in the fifth generation emigrated to Tenmile just after the war. The next generation, the sixth, migrated west yet again, to settle in eastern Ohio. Then, came even larger steps further west to Indiana, Illinois, Iowa, Wisconsin, and even entirely across the continent to the Pacific Northwest. The westward push was never really squelched until they reached the western continental shore, as did William[6ot] Van Buskirk on the Oregon Trail in 1852 and Joseph[8] Van Buskirk, who retired to California in the early 1900s. In my own eleventh generation, my sister Joan[11] and her family settled in California in the 1960s and, a decade or so later, my family and I settled in Oregon.

From our vantage point over two centuries after the Revolutionary War, we can only surmise the Van Buskirks' motivation for their post Revolutionary War western migration, but we can be sure that they weren't alone. After the French and Indian War, settlers began pouring into the new land between the Appalachians and the Mississippi River so much that the British government became wary. A royal proclamation of 1763 banned colonialists from crossing the Appalachian Mountains, but it was an ineffective deterrent that became moot with the onset of war. By the Revolutionary War's end, some 100,000 American settlers had migrated over those mountains. Opportunities to escape the aftermath of war, to obtain affordable land, and to achieve some elements of self-determination must have been among their reasons. Religious freedom undoubtedly contributed to the thinking of some, even if it was not their primary motivating factor. At least it would enable them to ride the tide of the many Pennsylvania Quakers and other pacifists who were escaping the war. Many northern Buck's County Quaker families crossed the Appalachians around 1780 to settle a sizable colony of Friends along the south bank of the South Tenmile Creek in Greene County, in the far southwest corner of Pennsylvania. Among them were Strawns, Johnsons, and Van Buskirks.[L]

The Quaker Friends were socially and numerically prominent in northern Buck's County. Their rolls included Van Buskirks as documented by civil and church records of that time.[L] As the pacifists among colonists who were revolting against British rule, the followers of Quaker Society of Friends confronted the intolerable dilemma of having to refuse service in the colonial militia or facing expulsion from their Quaker Society. We do not know exactly how the Van Buskirks came to grips with this situation, but we do know that they certainly were not pacifists. Despite their association with the Society of Friends, Joseph[5] Van Buskirk Sr., his father, four brothers, and at least one cousin all joined the Northampton Battalion Militia and fought against the British. Nonetheless, after the war, Joseph's[5] brother Lawrence[5], and two sisters, Sarah[5] and Susannah[5], each married into Quaker or "Quaker-leaning" families, and they each joined in the post-war Quaker migration to the Friends' colony along the South Tenmile Creek in Greene County (see fig. 11).

Figure 11. Pennsylvania Map, 1804 showing The Tenmile Country around Tenmile Creek. The region became Greene County in 1796. Map Source: Drawn by S. Lewis, engraved by D. Fairman, from Arrowsmith & Lewis's New and Elegant General Atlas, 1st ed.[AL] Although published in 1804, the map is dated 1800–1803 by counties shown, and the same identical map was published in all later editions of the atlas.

These early Van Buskirks appear to have been rather mercurial, perhaps opportunistic, in their religious preferences. Perhaps their association with the Society of Friends was more social than devoutly religious. They were relative latecomers to Buck's County and came not for religious reasons but because of the available property. Furthermore, the colony of New Netherlands had not been founded on religious grounds. From its beginning, the Dutch colony espoused, even if it did not always enforce, policies that welcomed people of all beliefs.[Sh] William Nelson, writing in the early 1900s, observed that our original progenitor, Laurens[1] Andriessen Van Buskirk, despite his influential positions in his regional Dutch and English society, never held any church office during his four decades in New York and New Jersey. Nelson suggests that this may be explained by his attendance in the Dutch Reform church despite being a Lutheran.[N]

Regardless, considering that the earlier generations of Van Buskirks had been German Lutheran or Dutch Reform in New Amsterdam, and that later, by the time they reached Ohio, they had become devout Presbyterians, they must not have been too committed to the Quaker doctrine. Similarly, Lackey reports that the Johnsons, whose son and daughter married Sarah[5] and Lawrence[5] Van Buskirk respectively, also were not strict members of the Friends but that they, too, were part of the western Quaker migration to the Tenmile colony in Greene County.[L] Lawrence[5], married Catherine Johnson in Northampton, Pennsylvania, before they migrated west to Greene County, Pennsylvania. Lawrence's sister Sarah[5] Van Buskirk married Nicholas Johnson, brother of Catherine; Susannah[5] Van Buskirk married Jacob Strawn II. They all settled and raised families among their Quaker neighbors along the Tenmile.[L]

Just as we have no definitive documentation for the reasons they decided to move west, we can, at best, only speculate about the method and route of their travels. Even at the time of their first contact with Europeans, the native North American people regularly trod their innumerable footpaths that crisscrossed what the Europeans believed to be an inland wilderness. After the colonial forts were built along riverbanks, the Indians would come down from the interior by these ancient pathways to meet and trade with settlers well before the Europeans had even considered establishing trails of their own. Eventually, the colonists did establish roadways by widening and strengthening these well-established Indian paths. At first, these early roadways were designed only to accommodate horses for a postal service between population centers like Boston, New York, and Charleston. Later, Britain's King Charles ordered that a wider through-roadway be built, the King's Highway, one that would connect all the colonies on the eastern seaboard. The route ultimately became strategically vital in both the French and Indian and the Revolutionary Wars.

After the King's Highway, one of the next earliest routes to be completed was the Lancaster Road that led west from Philadelphia to the Susquehanna River. This would have been a likely first leg of the Van Buskirk's journey across Pennsylvania. Just as they crossed the southern Pennsylvania border into Maryland, they would have encountered Braddock's Road that ran northwest from the Chesapeake to Fort Pitt. From Braddock's Road, their likely final leg would have been to branch west at Fort Necessity and head toward the Tenmile Country. There, a cutoff known as Gist's Trace had been created around 1790, approximating today's US Route 40[Do] (see fig. 12).

The Conestoga wagon was the most popular method of transport for the overland routes to the Shenandoah Valley and Western Pennsylvania, but Lackey reports that many simply walked or traveled on horseback or oxen, generally in large family groups. By end of the eighteenth century, there were carriage routes from Winchester, Virginia to the Tenmile country.[L]

Oddly, one reads wildly different tales about encounters with the native North American Indians along these trails. The indigenous people had been traversing the trails freely for centuries, often laying them out along ridge lines in the river valleys, high enough to avoid the flood plains but still protected by the valley walls. In the northern reaches of North America, the nations of the Iroquois were said to have been highly organized. They did their best

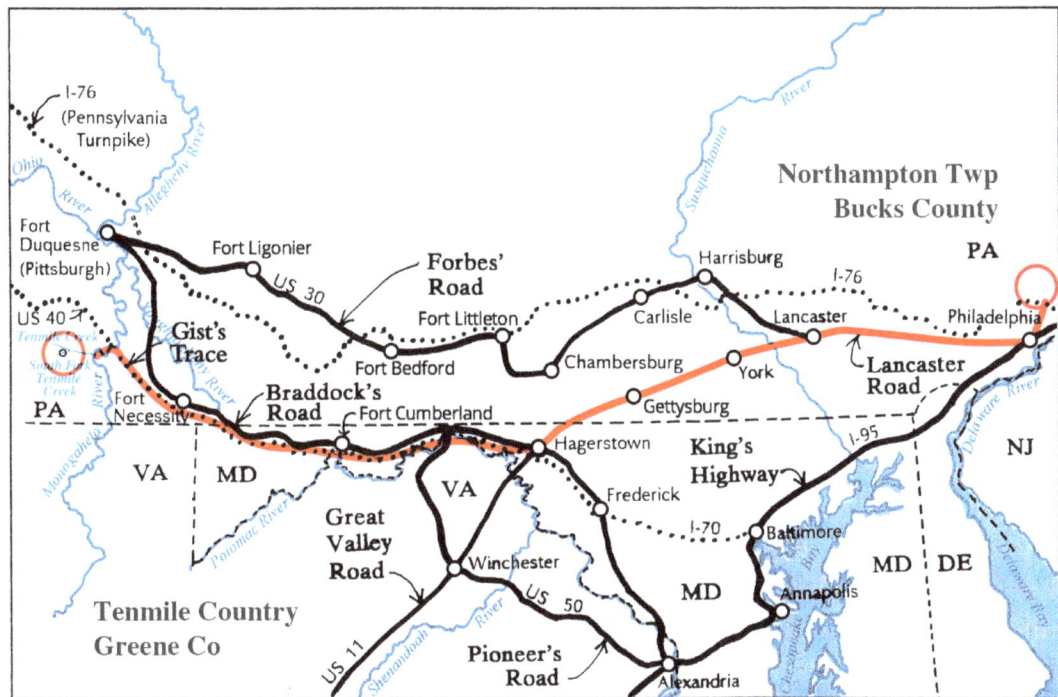

Figure 12. Possible migration route taken in 1812 across Pennsylvania by the Van Buskirk party from Bucks County to Greene County following the Lancaster Road to Braddock's Road to Gist's Trace. (Adapted from Map Guide to American Migration Routes, 1735–1815, 2002.[Do]*)*

to discourage western migration into the interior by European colonialists. Even as the first settlers arrived at Fort Orange in 1625, the Mohawk and Mahican Indians came down the rivers to meet and trade with Dutch settlers rather than encourage the newcomers to venture inland. By the late eighteenth century, firsthand descriptions among early settlers in the Ohio River Valley and western Pennsylvania describe relatively frequent and generally peaceful random encounters with Indians along the trails in those areas. According to one account, it was customary when meeting Indian travelers to sit a while, discuss local news, and perhaps share some food or a smoke before moving on. Of course, such interactions could be highly variable depending on local conditions, much as today we might have widely varying experiences encountering strangers in the night.

We can, again, only speculate about the motivations and pathways for the next stage of migration to Ohio, but there were plenty of incentives. At the end of the Revolutionary War, the new United States federal government looked to the relatively untapped land west of the Ohio River as an exceptionally attractive location in which to settle the many citizens displaced by the war. It also could serve as a potential source of much needed federal income. Thus, the Continental Congress began to examine alternatives for this public land. Four of the original colonies—Virginia, Massachusetts, Connecticut, and Pennsylvania—had prior claims to large sections of the region, but the congress ultimately persuaded those states of the newly constituted Union to give up their claims in order to facilitate the federal government. Despite the British ban on crossing the Appalachian Mountains, even before and during the war, a few settlers had managed to trickle into the Ohio country. Near the Delaware Indian village of Tuscarawi along the Tuscarawas River in eastern Ohio, Moravian missionaries had established a mission called Schoenbrun, where they had proselytized from the mid-1700s. The mission included creating a community of immigrants and converting the local Delaware Indians. Although the Delawares had agreed to be neutral in the war, both the Americans and the British suspected Schoenbrun of abetting the other side, and the mission was abandoned in 1778.[Hu]

The Continental Congress of 1784 passed the first of three Northwest Ordinances with subsequent revisions in 1785 and 1787. These provided that seven—later revised to five—territorial ranges would each become eligible for statehood when the population reached that of the least populous state. The citizens of the Northwest Territories were entitled to all rights and privileges of the original thirteen states. In addition, a bill of rights, forerunner to the federal Bill of Rights, amended to the federal constitution was provided, including the right to practice any religion and the prohibition of slavery within the Northwest Territories. After completion of the northwest territorial land survey, each territory was divided into six-mile square blocks, and each of these into thirty-six, one-mile square lots. The federal government would then sell this public land for a minimum of one dollar per acre. These arrangements made more sense to the government and new landholders than to the Indian people who had occupied the entire area for hundreds of years. It thus took a decade or two in order to establish sufficient relative security that would encourage many of the eastern settlers to venture west.

Beginning in 1800, land parcels were sold from the first land office in Steubenville, Ohio, on the Pennsylvania border, at two dollars per acre, for a minimum of 300 acres. The Steubenville land office stood just across the Ohio River from Greene County, Pennsylvania, and was the first successful one opened. The log building was constructed in 1801 and has been preserved to the present time.[F] The Van Buskirk cousins obtained land in Section 34 along the Indian Fork of One Leg Creek, a tributary of the Tuscarawas River in northeastern Ohio. Indian Fork was a branch of what is now Conotton Creek. In 1900, the creek was dammed to make Lake Atwood, now in Carroll and Tuscarawas counties submerging what had been the Van Buskirk farmlands.

Most of the pioneers in the early 1800s reached the Ohio country by traveling down the Ohio River by flatboat and up one of the many tributaries to their destination. Most of them carried a guidebook called *The Navigator*, by Zadoc Cramer, that presented details about river travel on the Monongahela, Allegheny, Ohio, and Mississippi rivers. Zadoc Cramer died in 1813, but the book was reprinted in multiple editions for many years after.

Because of the abundant water routes of the Ohio River, the Great Lakes, and numerous rivers running north and south between the two, Ohio had been a natural destination for pioneers and missionaries from the earliest days of the European exploration of North America. In addition, the Ohio territory, like Pennsylvania, was already carved with well-established Indian footpaths that allowed passage of local people and animals between the Ohio River and Lake Erie.

One such footpath, called The Great Trail, ran from the far western end of Lake Erie near what is now Detroit, Michigan, through the northern tip of what is now Tuscarawas County, to the Ohio River just at the northern tip of the present West Virginia Panhandle, approximated in later years by US Route 23. The Great Trail was in reality a complex network of ancient trails that the native Indians had used for transportation, communication, and trade.

During the war, The Great Trail had become a substantial transport route between the Great Lakes and the Chesapeake region and the site of repeated ambush and death, instilling rumors of being haunted by the ghosts of previous wars. One of the most famous episodes involved a Captain Lawrence[4] Van Buskirk. He was descended from Major Thomas[2] Van Buskirk, not Andries[2]. The following is excerpted from the "The Last Indian Battle on our Soil," Chapter VII, The Yellow Creek Stories, by Robert Schilling, and from genealogical information and commentary in Shoemaker[S, Sc]:

> Captain Lawson Van Buskirk was the commanding officer at Fort Decker near Mingo in 1782 . . . It was in the summer of 1792(1) that a large party of 28 Indians . . . passed down what is now Market Street in Steubenville to the Ohio River . . . where they hid their boats."[Sc]

As the story continues to relate, unfortunately, Mrs. (Van) Buskirk happened to be returning home on horseback from the weaver's when she encountered the Indian party. Her horse shied, throwing her to the ground. She severely sprained her ankle, and the Indians took her prisoner. At that point, three pioneer scouts happened along and attempted to pursue and rescue the hapless woman. The Indians, impeded by their hobbled captive, tomahawked her and escaped across the river in their boats. A few days later, a rescue party discovered her body. Eleven months after that, her husband, "Capt." (Van) Buskirk, organized thirty Indian fighters to obtain revenge but he, himself, was killed in the ensuing battle.[Sc] Shoemaker then makes her usual strong case that it was not actually Captain Van Buskirk to whom this all refers, but rather his son, Lieutenant Lawson (Lawrence)[5] Van Buskirk, whose wife, Rebecca, had been killed, and who had been killed himself as described in 1791. The father, Captain Van Buskirk, lived out the eighteenth century; his will was not proven until 1802.[S]

Thus, Joseph[6] Van Buskirk and his cousins cleared the land and settled into peaceful lives along the Indian Fork Creek in the Tuscarawa Valley. But, as Lackey predicted, the next generation would continued to move west, with James[7] and Jacob[7r] both moving on to eastern Indiana.[L] However, it was for the next generation of Van Buskirks who farmed a bit to the west in Knox County to make the ultimate western migration. William[6ot] Van Buskirk was the Joseph[6] Van Buskirk cousin who had settled in neighboring Knox County Ohio. He and his family, succumbing again to the sirens of the West, took the most ambitious journey of all, trudging the entire length of the infamous Oregon Trail as described in a later chapter.

CHAPTER 6

THE FIFTH GENERATION: JOSEPH VAN BUSKIRK (1751–1821) AND HIS SIBLINGS

AFTER THE REVOLUTIONARY WAR, four adult children of George[4] Van Buskirk emigrated from their home in Northampton, Pennsylvania, across the Appalachian Mountains to Maryland or southwest Pennsylvania. The remaining three children—Andrew[5], Daniel,[5] and Joseph[5]—remained behind on land their father had owned in Northampton Township of Bucks County, the first two of the brothers to farm, and Joseph[5] to run his inn.

The Fort Wayne branch of the Van Buskirk family traces its lineage through the third son of George[4] Van Buskirk, namely, Joseph[5] Van Buskirk, one of the three sons who, after the war, had remained behind in Northampton Township. Born in 1751, it was a rough and tumultuous, if interesting, time to grow up in a turbulent eighteenth-century North America. Joseph[5] Van Buskirk, his four brothers—John[5], Lawrence[5], Andrew[5], and Daniel[5]—as well as his father, George[4]—had all enlisted in the Northampton Militia to serve in the War of Independence. Around 1772, Joseph[5] married a Quaker woman named Mary Strawn. They had three children: William[6], Christiana[6], and Joseph[6]. After Mary's death in 1782, Joseph[5] married again, that time to Mary Levers (the sister of his oldest son's future wife), with whom he had five more children: Amelia[6], George[6] Levers, Robert[6], Charles[6], and Lynford[6]. After the war,

The Fifth Generation: Joseph Van Buskirk (1751–1821) and his Siblings.

Joseph[5] returned to Northampton where he kept an Inn until his death on May 31, 1821. His obituary of June 8, 1821 ("The Mountaineer," Easton, Pa.) described Joseph as "a worthy and respectable citizen." Beyond his service in the Northampton 4th Battalion Militia, most notable to our branch of the Van Buskirk extended family was that he was father to Joseph[6], who, by joining his uncles, aunts, and cousins in the Tenmile region, resumed our family's progressive migration west to Ohio and beyond. Joseph[6] would belatedly join the Van Buskirk migration to Greene County, Pennsylvania, just before their further move west.

By the time that the innkeeper Joseph[5] Van Buskirk, Sr. died at Northampton, Pennsylvania, on May 31, 1821, his older brothers and sisters, as well as his namesake son, Joseph[6], had long gone to the West.

CHAPTER 7

THE SIXTH GENERATION: JOSEPH VAN BUSKIRK (1782–1864)

Joseph^6 Van Buskirk, the second son and namesake of Pennsylvania innkeeper Joseph^5 and Mary (Strawn) Van Buskirk, was born April 20, 1782 in Northampton, Pennsylvania, just as the Revolutionary War was drawing to a close. Despite the Quaker leanings, or pretense, of the Van Buskirk family of that time, he was baptized in the Presbyterian Church.^{S} The family must have already suppressed what Quaker inclinations it might have had in prior years.

Joseph^6 Van Buskirk, son of Joseph^5, is sometimes confused in contemporary genealogical accounts with Joseph^{6b} Van Buskirk who was born six years earlier on February 23, 1776 and was the son of John^5 Van Buskirk, Joseph's^5 older brother. This Joseph^{6b}, had he lived, would have been Joseph's^6 first cousin. He was baptized on March 23, 1776 at the Church of Christ Church, but Shoemaker could find no more records of his existence. However, his father, John^5 Van Buskirk, who had moved immediately after the war to the Linton Hundred region of Maryland, had purchased a family bible with his son Lawrence. The family bible ultimately resided with the youngest son, William^{6ot}. John^5 filled in the blanks for births and deaths as if they had all been entered at the same time, as a group, undoubtedly long after the death of Joseph^{6b}. Later in the bible, the handwriting changes, presumably from John^5 to his William^{6ot}. This family

The Sixth Generation: Joseph VanBuskirk (1782–1864)

bible was carried by William[6ot] Van Buskirk on the Van Buskirk's arduous trek over the Oregon Trail, and it has been preserved by his direct descendants to the current time. The family pages from that bible, first inscribed in the late 1700s, are reproduced in Rosalie Viola Matthews Flint's family history book.[F1] John's[5] son Joseph[6b] died, and his death is therein recorded for September, 1779, at the age of only 3.[F1] In the same handwriting, presumably John's[5], he also lists the death of another son, Andrew, who died at the same time, September, 1779.[F1] Perhaps one of those virulent childhood illnesses of that time—maybe diphtheria or scarlet fever—had swept through the family. Shoemaker does not list Andrew as one of John's[5] children, but he is listed in the family bible as having been born on April 24, 1778.[S,F1] Thus, this old family bible confirms the tale of Joseph[6b], son of John[5] who has been subsequently so often confused with Joseph[6], the son of Joseph[5], described in these subsequent pages.

Around 1804, Joseph[6] Van Buskirk married Rebecca Villars in Northampton. Rebecca was the tenth child of John Villars of Greene County, Pennsylvania, who was a veteran of the Revolutionary War, having served with the Lieutenant William Wither's Rangers.[L] At least until 1811, Joseph[6] and Rebecca remained in eastern Pennsylvania, where they had five children. By 1812, they had emigrated to Greene County in southwestern Pennsylvania, but only for a short time until they joined Joseph's[6] cousins in their move to the Tuscarawas Valley.

Again, one must rely upon "informed speculation" to postulate about exactly what transpired among the families in the colony of Quaker Friends along the Tenmile Creek in Greene County and those who remained behind in Northampton Township, Bucks County. George's[4] son Joseph[5] had kept his inn in Northampton for the remainder of his life, but, like his siblings, he had married a Quaker woman, Mary Strawn, who was the daughter of Jacob Strawn, one of the original settlers of the Friends Colony in Green County. The Strawns descended from Lancelot Strawn (Straughan) who had emigrated from Wales to settle among the Quaker Friends in Buck's County, Pennsylvania, in the early 1700s. Lancelot's three sons, Thomas, John, and

Jacob all were among the original settlers of the Quaker colony along Tenmile Creek in western Pennsylvania. It is important to understand that although the Friends had established a settlement along the Tenmile Creek, the area was by no means exclusively Quaker. Many denominations had settled in the region.

Joseph's[5] sister Susannah[5] Van Buskirk married Jacob Strawn II, her mother's brother who, of course, was also from Greene County. Jacob and Susannah Strawn's son George Strawn then married Anne[6] Van Buskirk, who was the daughter of Lawrence[5] and Catherine Van Buskirk. Three of Joseph's[5] siblings—Lawrence[5], Catherine[5], and Susannah[5]—all moved back to Greene County after they were married. As the final connection, Joseph's[5] son Joseph[6], born in 1782, met and ultimately married Rebecca Villars who was the daughter of John Villars, also of Greene County. Thus, despite the long and formidable physical distances between, there must have been considerable communication between the Friends' communities in Greene County and Buck's County, Pennsylvania, during the post-war period and probably before.

Before moving to Greene County, Joseph[6] and Rebecca (Villars) Van Buskirk raised five children in eastern Pennsylvania, of whom the last was James[7], born September 4, 1811. Once they reached the Tenmile country, they promptly, in 1812, joined their cousins on a further arduous emigration, this time across and down the Ohio River to the Tuscarawas Valley in northeastern Ohio. In all, at least six Van Buskirk families of the grandchildren of George[4] Van Buskirk eventually migrated to the Tuscarawas River valley in eastern Ohio. These included two sons and one daughter of Lawrence[5] Van Buskirk—Lawrence[6], Nicholas[6], and Mary[6] (Van Buskirk) Strawn—as well as three sons of Joseph[5] Van Buskirk—Joseph[6], Charles[6], and Lynford[6]. The latter two, Charles[6] and Lynford[6] were much younger stepbrothers to Joseph[6], born to Joseph's[5] second wife, Mary Levers. They were young children at the time of the 1812 original emigration to Ohio, but they both came later around 1820. Both married women in Ohio.

The Sixth Generation: Joseph VanBuskirk (1782-1864)

By 1812, Joseph's[5] older brother, Lawrence[5], and Lawrence's[5] wife, Catherine Van Buskirk, had become well established along Tenmile Creek in Greene County and remained there for the rest of their lives. Their sons, Nicholas[6], born 1781, and Lawrence[6], born 1789, were raised along the Tenmile Country and married, Anne Elizabeth Cree, and Sarah Richardson respectively. But as their parents had done after the Revolutionary War, they too began to look for opportunities in the West. Eventually, with their sister Anne[6], her husband, George Strawn, and their cousin Joseph[6] (our direct ancestor), they all embarked upon another great migration west. They eventually settled on adjacent farms in the Tuscarawas Valley of Ohio.

Nicholas's[6] wife, Anne Elizabeth (Cree) was, perhaps, among the first doctors in the region. Such women like Anne Elizabeth were known as "root doctors." At that time there were no medical colleges in the area and, in any event, female attendance at medical colleges was frowned upon. The healing and midwifery arts commonly fell to women who learned their skills from other women and from the local native people. They fulfilled an important role in the pioneer social fabric. Several of the Van Buskirk estate documents from Tuscarawas County in the early 1800s refer to her as Dr. Anne E. Van Buskirk. One cannot help but wonder if she had been the inspiration to her male cousins and nephews that spawned a passion for medicine that lasted through the four subsequent generations.

We do not know the exact route or means by which they traveled, but it would have been possible to travel the 60 or so miles from Tenmile Creek in Pennsylvania to Steubenville overland by wagon following the continuation of Gist's Trace to the Ohio River. From there, they likely would have traveled downstream from Steubenville on the Ohio River by flatboat, and then up the Muskingum River to the Tuscarawas River, but that is nothing but educated speculation (see fig. 13).

The Van Buskirk party from Greene County seems to have traversed the wilderness uneventfully and arrived safely in the Tuscarawas Valley of Ohio

Figure 13. Possible Routes from the Tenmile Area to Tuscarawas Valley, overland via Gist's Trace to the Ohio River and by flat boat from there. Map shown is a composite image from various sources with reference points added by the author.

in 1812. Joseph[6] acquired a large farm in Section 34, Tuscarawas County, on the Indian Fork alongside his cousins. Most of their other Ohio neighbors were German or Irish: Elliott, McKee, Cellars, Finley, and Gray were among the most frequently recurring surnames intermixing with the various Van Buskirks in the region (see fig. 14). On the detritus of the past, on certificates of birth and death, marriage licenses, wills, deeds, and church records, their names intertwine like the vines on their tombstones. Charles[6] Van Buskirk married Mary Ann McKee on December 27, 1821 in Tuscarawas County.

The Sixth Generation: Joseph VanBuskirk (1782-1864)

After Mary died in 1847, Charles[6] married Elizabeth Neighbors on June 6, 1847. After Charles died in 1855, his brother Lynford[6] married his brother's widow, Elizabeth (Neighbors) Van Buskirk. As the families intermarried, they shared a relatively isolated pioneer life.

Joseph[6] and Rebecca already had five children at the time of their migration west in 1812, including their infant son, James[7], who was born in Northampton

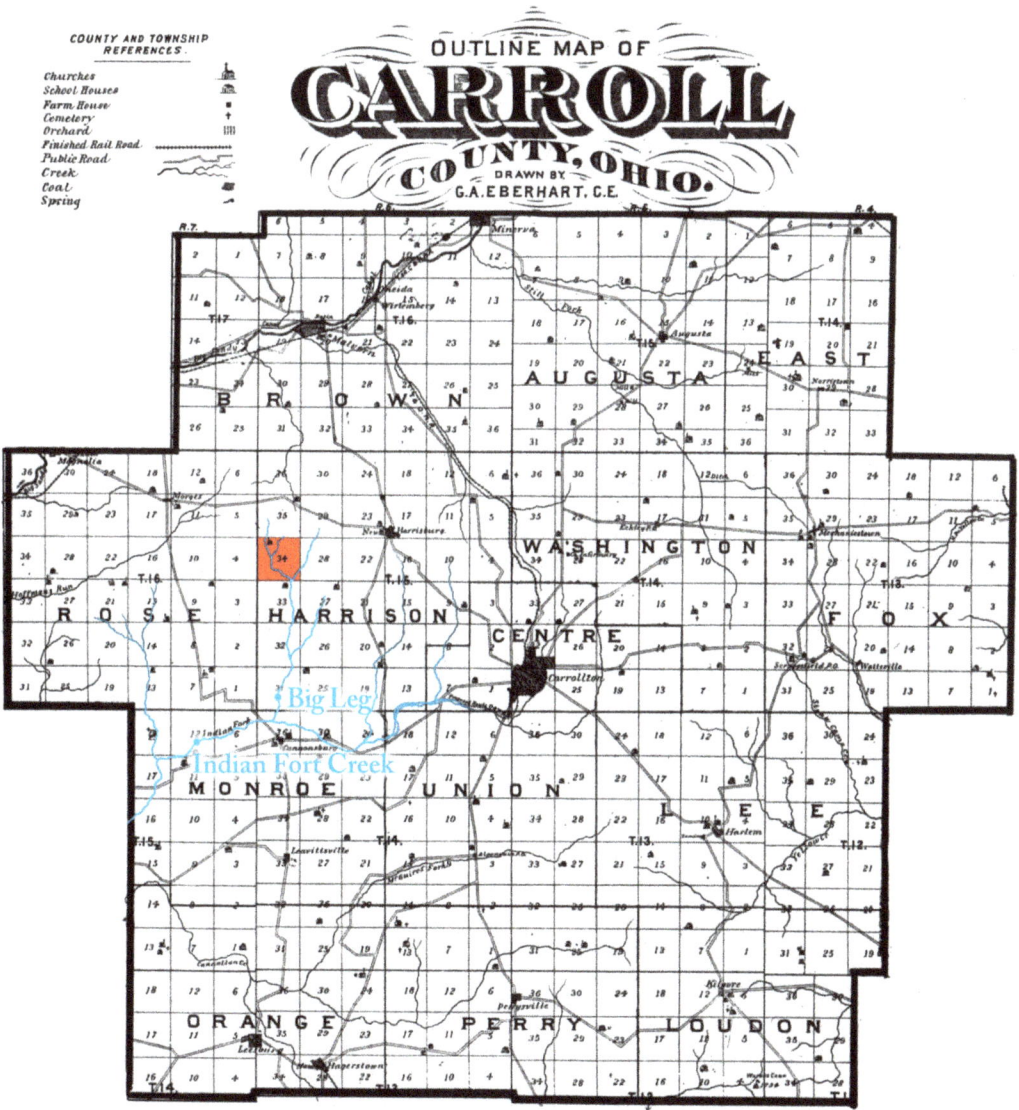

Figure 14. Carroll County Section 34, delineated (in red) as per H.H. Hardesty, Illustrated Historical Atlas—Carroll County, Ohio.[H] *When the Van Buskirks settled on Indian Fork in 1812, it was originally in Tuscarawas County but became Carroll County in 1832.*

Township, Pennsylvania, on September 4, 1811. Their next child, George[7], born in 1813, became the first born to their new Ohio home. He must have been one of the earliest babies born to the colonial settlement: the first settler birth in the region had taken place only four years earlier in 1809.[H] The last of their twelve children were twins born August 31, 1825, Elizabeth[7] and Jacob[7r]. Rebecca died only five years later in 1830.

Jacob[7r] married Mary Ann Elliott, the daughter of neighbor Aaron Elliott, a close friend and associate of Joseph[6]. Their son, Aaron[8r] Elliott Van Buskirk (later called "A.E."), named for his maternal grandfather, eventually moved to Fort Wayne, Indiana and became a well-known physician there.

By the same token, James's[7] son Joseph[8] likewise became a physician, but he wound up in Rapid City, South Dakota. James's[7] son Linford[8], my great-grandfather, also moved to Allen County, Indiana, where he had a large farm in Monroeville, but his son, my grandfather and namesake, became a prominent physician in Fort Wayne as well.

After his wife's death in 1830, Joseph[6] married twice more but had no additional children. The Deep Springs Church remained the social and religious focus for Van Buskirks and Elliotts, with both Joseph[6] and Aaron Elliott serving on the board of elders for much of their adult years and buried in Deep (Big) Springs Cemetery, their graves separated by perhaps 100 feet. Despite his arduous pioneer life, Joseph[6] Van Buskirk lived to the age of 82, dying on May 30, 1864. Theirs was a difficult life from the beginning, perhaps more so than for their pioneer parents.

CHAPTER 8

PIONEER LIFE IN EASTERN OHIO

Even as late as 1822, Hardesty describes only "a few cleared patches" among the nearly unbroken forests of eastern Ohio.[H] Of course, it is now well understood that the dense forests did not preclude a complex social organization among North American Indians who had intermittently occupied the territory preceding the hardy pioneers by many centuries.[M] Joseph[6] and Rebecca Van Buskirk and their cousins established themselves along the Indian Fork of One Leg Creek, a tributary of the Tuscarawas River in what is now Tuscarawas County. They were farmers, but the land was heavily forested and needed to be cleared, tree by tree, rock by rock. Wild game constituted the principal meat of their diet. Life centered around clearing and farming the land, building homes, hunting for game, protecting the homestead, and the community of neighbors and church. The first schoolhouse was built of logs in Brown Township, 16' x 18' in size, with joists so low that the taller scholars could clasp their hands around them. Houses were generally made of logs and a few have been preserved to the current time, as described by Firestone.[F]

Life was arduous but generally peaceful. Wild animals, especially bears, wolves, and deer were very common, posing both a threat and a source of meat. Cooperation among the settlers generally marked the day with very little crime. Despite the establishment of a court system in the state of Ohio by the early 1800s, in the eastern pioneer settlements, most crime and other transgressions were mediated by the community church, not by a formal court of justice. Witches were executed as late as 1825. No markets for buying or selling of goods existed in the region, the nearest being in Steubenville, 50 miles away. Exchange of property, goods, and services, for the most part, took place between individuals. Salt was so scarce one man exchanged his prize steer for a barrel.[H] Although the farms that could produce abundant crops comprised the principal industry, the long distances and high cost of shipping precluded any significant market beyond their immediate neighbors. Thus, in general, the communities became self-sufficient, with their residents growing and hunting for themselves in the early years; all able-bodied men worked by the sweat of their brow, managing their farms, hunting, and providing for their families.

What little leisure available was centered around the church. The more cerebral activities like teaching and doctoring were not for workingmen but were left to women, like Dr. Anne Elizabeth (Cree) Van Buskirk, or the lame or aged who were not able to perform regular hard labor.

By the time they were settled in Ohio, the Van Buskirks and their new neighbors established the Deep Springs Presbyterian Church near their own homes along the same creek. (The creek was dammed during the 1900s, destroying the church, but the cemetery was restored along the bank of the dam reservoir.) By 1838, the church was sufficiently surfeit with Van Buskirks, Elliotts, McKees, and Cellars to hire a permanent minister. The devout paid a few dollars each month to cover the minister's salary, but they often fell behind in their payments, as recorded in the church minutes, requiring Joseph Van Buskirk or Aaron Elliott to collect the fees. Their severe life cut little slack. The minutes of church meetings of February 21, 1825—at which Aaron Elliott, James Cellars, and Joseph[6] Van Buskirk served as Church Elders—report the calling before the church a woman named Hannah Mills. The woman stood accused by a sister parishioner, Katherine Hunt, of selling two guinea fowls on the Sabbath. Van Buskirk and Elliott both questioned to submission the poor

Mrs. Mills who was "churched"—drummed out or excommunicated—from the congregation to face the ostracism of the tightly knit neighbors.

County lines rapidly changed with new pioneer settlements in the early 1800s in Ohio. In 1800 there were only nine counties, but sixteen by the time of statehood in 1803 and over forty by 1812, the year Joseph[6] arrived. So quickly did the county lines change, that one innkeeper, Joseph Cellars, whose son had married Joseph's[6] daughter Mary[7] Van Buskirk, suddenly found his establishment straddling the new county line. To make matters worse, one of the new counties banned the sale of alcoholic beverages and the innkeeper found his bar on the dry side of the line! The enterprising Cellars had little recourse but to rearrange his furniture by moving his bar across the county line to the other side of the room thus complying with both the spirit and letter of the law. Many of the citizenry were conflicted between the Methodist ban on alcohol consumption and the local custom, whereby most social and even legal contracts such as weddings and property sales were sealed and sanctified with a gulp of whiskey from the jug. For even the most informal visit, to withhold the jug was unneighborly at best, insulting at worse.

By the middle of the nineteenth century, some of the cities of Ohio, especially Cincinnati, had become fairly cosmopolitan, but the rural lands of Ohio continued to demand a harsh way of pioneer life.

CHAPTER 9

THE SEVENTH GENERATION: JAMES VAN BUSKIRK

(1811–1869)

James[7] Van Buskirk was the fifth child of Joseph and Rebecca (Villars) Van Buskirk, and the last of Joseph and Rebecca's children to be born in Northampton County, Pennsylvania (September 4, 1811). James[7] travelled, likely by wagon, as a babe-in-arms, first to Greene County, Pennsylvania, and shortly thereafter, in 1812, from Greene County to the valley of Ohio's Tuscarawas River. As noted before, the family found a remarkably unsettled land of scattered log cabins along Indian trails and pristine creeks and rivers.

The pioneers generally favored river travel, but the shoreline was not always free from hostile Native American Indians who must have wondered why these foreign people had come to settle in their lands. Settle they did, however, living relatively peacefully among their Indian neighbors. James[7] grew up helping his father, siblings, and cousins clear the land and establish their farms. The Van Buskirks and the other emigrants from the East had built their little pioneer village and lived within the rigid confines of the Deep Springs Presbyterian Church community as described in the previous chapter.

Life was hard for James[7] and his siblings on the frontier farm in eastern Ohio. By the 1830s, the threat from large game and native uprisings had, by and large, disappeared, but pestilence pervaded the land in the form of yellow fever, scarlet fever, malaria, and tuberculosis. Whether from exhaustion or disease, James's[7] mother, Rebecca, died in 1830. His oldest brother, John[7], died at the age of 25. Throughout the settling of the frontier, pioneers tended to establish their communities along riverbanks as the most accessible locations in the wilderness. Lying as they did in damp lowlands, these were not the healthiest spots where they could have chosen to live. The marshy lands were rife with mosquitoes, stagnant infested ponds and swampland. Malaria and yellow fever were rampant along their riverbanks; nearly half of the workers and passengers along the Wabash and Erie Canal died from the miasmic pestilence engulfing them. One pioneer in Illinois told of mosquitoes on a summer evening so thick that when he held his arm out for a few moments and then quickly withdrew it, the swarm left a hole, a negative cast in the cloud of insects!

By 1832, young James[7], 21, married Ann Morrow in Carroll County where they lived and farmed until 1850. James[7] and Annie had eleven children—seven girls and four boys—while living in Ohio. James's[7] brother George[7], the first Van Buskirk born in Ohio (September 17, 1813), married Annie's sister, Jane Morrow. In 1850, whether for reasons economic, cultural or health, James[7] and Annie, like the Van Buskirks before them, picked up their things and moved west, this time to Adams County, then Allen County, Indiana. His brother Jacob[7r], already ill, also lived briefly in Adams County before moving on with his young family to Aledo, Illinois, where he died in 1857.

James[7] Van Buskirk bought a rather sizable farm near Monroeville, Indiana, on the southern border of Allen County. In the year 2002, my daughter Sarah and I drove around the area and photographed the old farm (see fig. 15). I recall visiting the farm as a young child with my grandfather, Edmund[9] Michael Van Buskirk, James's[7] grandson. My grandfather drove me out to the family farm in his business coupe so that we could dig potatoes from his potato patch. In the process of digging for the potatoes, he used to find many flint arrowheads, many of which remain in our family.

Figure 15. Madison Township farmland photographed by the author in 2002 at the site of James[7] Van Buskirk's farm.

In all, James[7] and Annie Morrow Van Buskirk had thirteen children, nine girls and four boys. James[7] Van Buskirk, my great-great-grandfather, is the first of my direct ancestors of whom I have a portrait (see portrait 1). Their sixth daughter, Sarah[8], died at the age of 3 in Ohio. Elizabeth[8] was born in February 1850, and was the last of their children to be born in Ohio. After a brief return to eastern Pennsylvania, the family moved permanently to Indiana. There, they had two more daughters, Ellenora[8] in 1852, and Jemima[8] in 1856. James's[7] first son, George[8], was born in 1843 but died in the Civil War Battle of Gettysburg on July 7, 1863 (see portrait 2). His second son, Joseph[8], was raised in Monroeville and also fought in the Civil War, but with an Ohio unit. In May 1862, at the age of 18, Joseph[8] returned to Ohio and enlisted in Company D of the 88th Ohio Volunteer infantry.

The Seventh Generation: James Van Buskirk (1811–1869)

Unlike his older brother, Joseph[8] survived his stint in the war and returned to Monroeville where he taught school and worked for a sawmill. In 1864, he went to Appleton, Wisconsin where he matriculated at Lawrence University, and he received a bachelor degree in medicine. He then served a kind of medical preceptorship in Reedsburg, Wisconsin, before studying medicine at the University of Michigan. In 1872, he finally received his doctor of medicine (MD) degree from the Chicago Medical College. Joseph[8] Van Buskirk practiced medicine first in Reedsburg, Wisconsin, and then, briefly, in a variety of communities in the west, including Crook City in the Black Hills of South Dakota; in 1884, he practiced and also owned a drug store in Idaho. Ultimately the bachelor, Joseph[8], settled in Rapid City, South Dakota, where he continued to practice medicine until his retirement in the early twentieth century. He then retired to Long Beach, California where he died in 1915. He is buried in the Long Beach Municipal Cemetery.

James's[7] tenth and last son, Linford[8] (see portrait 4), my great-grandfather, was born in 1847, also in Ohio, and grew up to become an Indiana farmer in Monroeville until his death in 1910.

James's[7] first wife, Annie (Morrow) Van Buskirk, died in Root, Indiana, in 1860. The following year, on August 22, 1861, James[7] married Rebecca Pitters, who was some fifteen years younger than he was. They had three children, all girls: Ruth[8], born 1862; Etta[8], born 1864; and Rachel[8], born 1865. Four years later, in 1869, James[7] Van Buskirk died in Monroeville, Indiana. He is buried on the outskirts of the little town, in the Brown Family Cemetery. My daughter Sarah and I meticulously searched for and ultimately located that little cemetery, which lies seemingly forgotten on the edge of a farm (see fig. 16). There we found many neglected graves, some partially flooded in standing ground water, and others, overgrown with weeds and nettles. Most of the headstones were barely readable, many broken. We could not locate James's[7] stone. Happily, in the interim, the local Boy Scout troop has taken on restoration of the cemetery as a project: they have found

James's[7] stone, broken in half, but they have repaired and restored it to its proper location. There were many Van Buskirks who lived in the Monroeville area, as well as, of course, in the larger city of Fort Wayne. Many of James's[7] children and grandchildren are buried in the Monroeville Memorial Cemetery; only James[7] is interred at the Brown Family Cemetery.

After James[7] died, his widow remained in Root, Indiana, and, on August 12, 1877, married a man named George S. Cline. Rebecca died in 1889 in Root. In his last will, James[7] Van Buskirk left his house and surrounding property to his wife, Rebecca, and the young daughters he had had with her. His will called for the remainder of his estate to be sold and the proceeds divided among his remaining children, including his son Linford[8], my great-grandfather.

Figure 16. Brown Family Cemetery, 2002, in a neglected and derelict state with broken tombstones overgrown with brambles and weeds amid sunken flooded areas. Recently, local boy scouts have restored the graveyard. They also located and restored James[7] Van Buskirk's stone. (Photo from the author's private collection.)

The Seventh Generation: James Van Buskirk (1811–1869)

Portrait 1. Top left: James⁷ Van Buskirk, 1811–1869. Signed Drawing.

Portrait 2. Top right: George⁸ Van Buskirk, 1843–July 7, 1863, brother to Linford⁸. Killed at Gettysburg.

Portrait 3. Left: Joseph⁸ Van Buskirk, MD, 1844–1915.

(Portraits from the author's private collection.)

CHAPTER 10

THE EIGHTH GENERATION: LINFORD VAN BUSKIRK

(1847–1910)

AMONG THE THIRTEEN CHILDREN of James[7] and Annie Van Buskirk, my great-grandfather Linford[8] Van Buskirk was born July 4, 1847 in Carroll County, Ohio, just a few years before the family moved to Indiana. At his father's death, Linford[8] inherited his share of the proceeds from the sale of the residual estate after the sale of his father's farm in Monroeville. Linford[8] married Mary (Maria) E. Knouse of Fort Wayne on April 26, 1874. (A green book of Knouse genealogy stands alongside the Van Buskirk tomes in our family library.)[K] The following year, Linford[8] received from the Knouse family one-fifth of a large lot in Section 24 of Madison Township, Allen County, near Monroeville where he and Mary lived, farmed, and prospered until his death in 1910. The plat map of Madison Township in 1878 shows the property divided between D Knouse (12/15) and L Van Buskirk (3/15) (see fig. 17).

Linford[8] and Mary are the eldest direct ancestors of whom I recall my father speaking. My father's grandfather Linford[8] died in 1910 when my father was only 3, but his grandmother Mary lived another twelve years until June 5, 1922—well within his direct memory. Oddly, neither Linford[8] nor his wife left a will. I believe that he must have given the farm property either to his wife or his children during his lifetime because the land, Section 24, eventually ended

The Eighth Generation: Linford Van Buskirk (1847–1910)

up with his son and daughter, Otis and Ella, as shown in the Plat Map of the 1930s (see fig. 17).

My father spoke often of his grandmother Mary and of his visits to her Monroeville Farm as though they were among the more vivid and, I thought, pleasant of his childhood memories. Mary Knouse was descended from a prominent Allen County family, Daniel and Maria Sterner Knouse. Through her mother, Maria Sterner Knouse, Mary Knouse was directly descended from another Revolutionary War veteran, Sergeant Casper Sterner. Mary's oldest brother, Aaron L. Knouse, was born on June 8, 1835 and died on September 8, 1858 while studying for the ministry near Chicago. Aaron Knouse is buried in

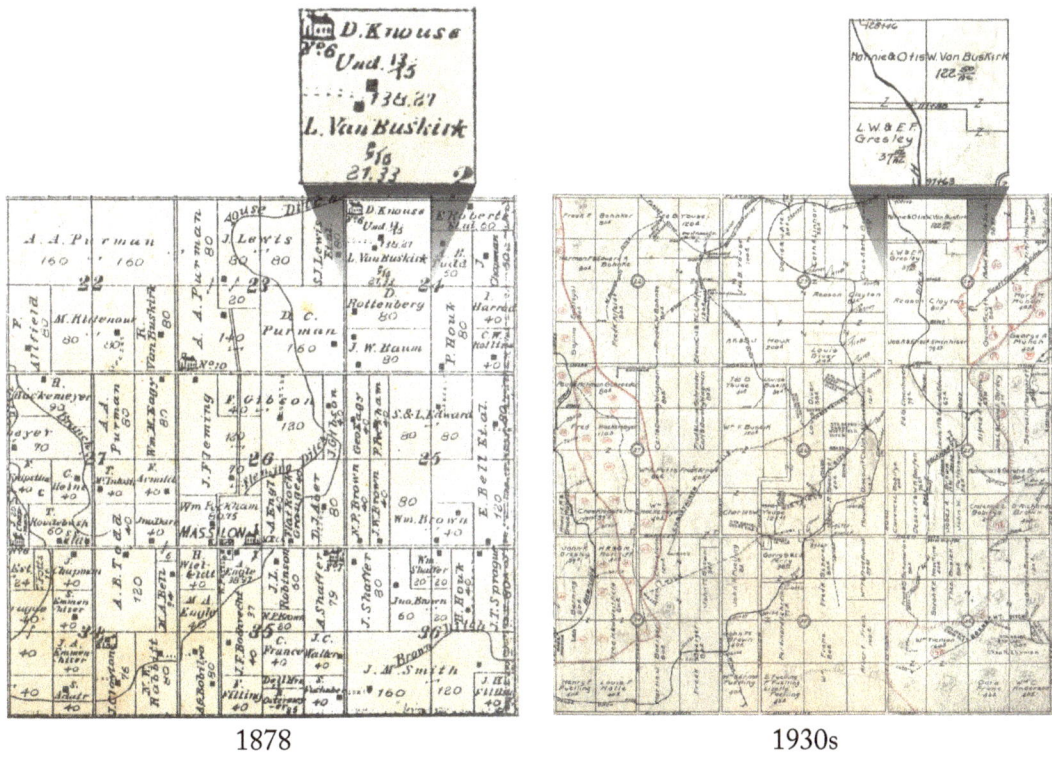

Figure 17. Plat Maps showing NW Quarter, Section 24 of Madison Township, Allen County, Indiana in 1878 with Linford and Mary Knouse Van Buskirk Farms, and in the 1930s with Otis Van Buskirk and Ella Van Buskirk Gresley on the same land. The Van Buskirk property is enlarged in both plat maps to show the owners. (Map copied from Allen County, Indiana, records, accessed at Fort Wayne Public Library.)

Monroeville, although not in the Monroeville Memorial Cemetery where the Van Buskirks are buried but rather in the Masonic Cemetery on the outskirts of the town. Her brother David S. Knouse, born May 10, 1837, served as Captain for the Union Army in the Civil War and survived the war. He immigrated west to Kansas where he worked as carpenter until his death on March 25, 1896. My father fondly recalled his grandmother Mary as a grand, but stern, farm matron.

On their farm in Monroeville, Indiana, Linford[8] and Mary raised four children, two boys and two girls: Edmund[9] Michael, Otis[9] Walter, Ella[9] Florilla (Gresley), and Ethel[9] May (Laudahn). The eldest, Edmund[9] Michael Van Buskirk, was my grandfather and namesake. Despite the intervening two-thirds of a century, I remember him well. All four siblings remained in the Fort Wayne area for the remainder of their lives. Like his father, Otis[9] became a farmer and farmed the same family land in Monroeville. Ella[9] Florilla married Leo Gresley, who also had a farm in Monroeville where they eventually farmed the same land as her father, Section 24 in Madison Township (see fig. 17). Ella's[9] sister, Ethel[9] May, married Frank Laudahn, a local man described in the federal census as a laborer, also in Monroeville.

Linford[8], Mary, and their four children all attended a large family reunion around the mid-1880s and assembled for a large group photograph (see fig. 18). I presume this was a reunion of Mary Knouse's or even the Sterner's family, both prominent and numerous in Allen County at that

Portrait 4. Linford[8] Van Buskirk, 1847–1910. (Photo from the author's private collection.)

time. Linford⁸, Mary, and all of their family are buried in the Monroeville Memorial Cemetery (also known as the IOOF Cemetery of Monroeville), except Edmund⁹ Michael, whose family plot is at the Lindenwood Cemetery in the city of Fort Wayne.

Figure 18. Family Reunion, ca. 1885. Circles from left to right:
1. Mary (Knouse) Van Buskirk, wife of Linford⁸ Van Buskirk; 2. Ethel⁹ Van Buskirk; 3. Ella⁹ Van Buskirk; 4. Linford⁸ Van Buskirk; 5. Edmund⁹ Michael Van Buskirk; 6. Otis⁹ Van Buskirk. The handwritten annotation for Edmund⁹ Michael appears to read "Dr. Van Buskirk," leading me to the presumption that it is as indicated. I suspect that this is either a Knouse or a Sterner family reunion. (Photo from the author's private collection.)

CHAPTER 11

THE NINTH GENERATION: EDMUND MICHAEL VAN BUSKIRK

(1875-1950)

My grandfather, Edmund[9] Michael Van Buskirk, was born in Monroeville, Allen County, Indiana, on February 11, 1875. He attended his local village school. Remarkably, as a very young man, barely in his teens, he set off to Chicago where he attended Jefferson High School, on the north side of Chicago, in order to complete his high school education. The Monroeville School did offer a high school curriculum, but he (or his parents) must have wanted a broader range of courses for him. It may also be that after graduation from Monroeville High School, he went to the Jefferson School in Chicago to obtain further education. I do recall my father telling me the story that my grandfather had attended school in Chicago and that, afterward, he had taught school back home in Monroeville. He was an avid teacher and student all of his life as evidenced by the memories and lore he left behind, as well as by his leather-bound books in Latin and Greek that now reside on my bookshelves.

Eventually, Edmund[9] Michael Van Buskirk matriculated at the Fort Wayne Medical College from which he graduated in 1902 (see fig. 19). As detailed in subsequent pages, the little proprietary medical college was founded in the 1870s and had a successful, albeit sometimes tumultuous, tenure in Fort Wayne until its closing in the early 1900s. The school even sported a football team of

The Ninth Generation: Edmund Michael Van Buskirk (1875-1950)

Figure 19. Fort Wayne College of Medicine, 1900, faculty and students photographed with the college in the background. Edmund⁹ Michael Van Buskirk stands in back row, wearing a flat-topped cap and looking to his right. Aaron⁸ʳ Elliott Van Buskirk, MD, Professor of Surgical Anatomy is seated, front row, middle, with a gray beard. (From the family's private collection.)

which my grandfather was the manager! (See fig. 20.) He served as a resident physician at the Indiana State School for the Feeble Minded. He then went to Boston to undertake additional training at Harvard University School of Medicine.

At first, the newly-minted physician entered private general practice in Fort Wayne, but very early on began to study the new field of X-ray or "roentgenology," as it was then most commonly known. He ultimately became one of the first radiologists in Indiana, a diplomat of the American Board of

Figure 20. Football Team, Fort Wayne College of Medicine, 1902. Edmund⁹ Michael Van Buskirk, Manager, second row from the top, in the white sweater. (From the family's private collection.)

Radiology, and a member of multiple national and local radiological societies. As early as 1905, he became a county health officer and developed a lifelong propensity for politics, at least within his own medical profession. In 1937, he served on the Indiana State Board of Health. By 1905, he was already a member of the Indiana State Medical Association, and just four years later, in 1909, was elected president of the 12th Indiana District Medical Society. He served as a captain in the U.S. Army Medical Corps during World War I (see portrait 7), and ultimately, he became president of the Indiana State Medical Association in 1938 (see portraits 8 and 9). Among his papers, I found an old manuscript, perhaps for an article or speech he was to give, describing the evils of "socialized medicine." Irene Shoemaker lists seven articles authored by him that were published in learned national medical journals.[S]

Edmund⁹ Michael's distinctive, old "shingle" sign depicting "Dr. Van Buskirk" in reverse painting on glass, first hung on the street in front of his office a century ago; today, it hangs in my study (see fig. 21).

The great irony of my grandfather's life, at least to me, was that, because he took up radiology in the infancy both of his own career and of the radiological medical field as a whole, he did not protect himself adequately from repeated exposure to x-rays before it was too late. He developed a severe aplastic anemia that ultimately killed him in 1950. I recall our family anecdote of how he routinely napped on his treatment table before beginning his afternoon schedule, but surely the machine would have been turned off.

Despite the intervening decades, I have clear memories of my grandfather in their home on Maxine Drive in Fort Wayne, Indiana, as well as the previously mentioned trips to the farm, but I have no memories of him being sick until the very end (see fig. 22). I do have obscure recollections of him having to receive blood transfusions, and I remember that, when I was an 8-year-old boy, our family, having received an urgent call from Fort Wayne, rushing the 100-mile drive across the state from Lafayette to his deathbed in Fort Wayne. After some preliminaries, we went to the hospital in Fort Wayne for what was to be the last time I would see him. I retain the child's vivid image, permanently seared upon my sensorium, of my grandfather's portrait in oil hanging in the hospital lobby, just opposite the entrance, like those one sees in public buildings of a president or a king. I thought he must be very important, but I had no idea

Figure 21. Edmund⁹ Michael Van Buskirk's reverse painting on glass "shingle" from his Fort Wayne office, early twentieth century. (From the family's private collection.)

why. Perhaps it was simply a matter that he was president or past president of the medical staff. I was taken to his room. He was alert and spoke briefly to me through the walls of a thin transparent plastic enclosure draped over the upper part of his bed—an "oxygen tent," as I later learned from my father.

I slept that night on Grandma Van's narrow daybed in a side room in their house that was filled to capacity with my family members. I recall, as if it were last week, not sixty-eight years ago in February 1950, that my mother awakened me in the morning with the sad news that Grandpa Van had died. My sister Nancy has related to me that she, ten years my elder, had been with him when he died and that it had been in the late afternoon. I suspect that my parents had decided to allow me to sleep the night before giving me the sad news in the morning.

I also recall my grandfather's body, lying "in state" in the sunroom off their living room in the house on Maxine Drive. Mournful visitors dropped by for what seemed to be several days, to view his now still body in that sun-struck, somber room. That solarium never again felt the same to me. But, though I was young, I knew he had lived an extraordinary life. As written in his obituary, only a few hours intervened from his final work in his office to entering the hospital as a terminally ill patient. I recall my father telling me "Grandpa had called his own shot," working to the last possible moment, and accurately predicting the day on which he would die.

Edmund[9] Michael Van Buskirk married Mary Louise Schwarze of Fort Wayne on January 10, 1906. They had two children, my father, Edmund[10] Linford Van Buskirk, born October 15, 1907, and Alice[10] Louise Van Buskirk, born June 29, 1911. Shoemaker devotes two pages of text to my grandfather.[S] Throughout his adult life he devoted much of his own spare time and energy collecting, in the most thorough and arduous manner, genealogical data about the Van Buskirk heritage. His work, in the pre-internet age, provided me my first exposure to Laurens[1] Andriessen from data ultimately given to Mrs. Shoemaker by my grandmother. We retained either originals or copies of many of those documents, the very ones that my father passed on to me shortly before his death in 1995. Edmund's[9] widow, my grandmother Mary Louise (Schwarze) Van Buskirk, lived another eleven years in the same house on Maxine Drive in Fort Wayne (see fig. 22). I recall her as a small woman, somewhat severe and strict but exceedingly kind. As a child, I would sometimes stay in Fort Wayne with my grandparents when my parents would travel for medical meetings. I remember her taking me to a big department store in Fort Wayne to see the Lionel trains! Oddly, after her husband's death, she drove to the bank every day, I suppose to get the money needed for that day and sometimes to "clip

Figure 22. Home on Maxine Drive, Fort Wayne, Indiana, that once belonged to my grandparents Edmund[9] Michael and Mary Louise Van Buskirk, photographed in 2002, over 40 years after my grandmother's death. (From the family's private collection.)

a coupon." One morning, while backing her car from her garage, she suffered a stroke and hit the side of the door. The same determination and fortitude that characterized her life allowed her failing mind and body to somehow stop the car in the driveway before she lost consciousness. She never regained her previously abundant faculties; she died in a nursing home some months later. Edmund[9] Michael Van Buskirk and Mary Louise (Schwarze) Van Buskirk are buried in a large family plot of the Lindenwood Cemetery in Fort Wayne, Indiana (see fig. 23).

Figure 23. Gravestone of Edmund[9] Michael and Mary Louise Van Buskirk at Lindenwood Cemetery, Fort Wayne, Indiana. (From the family's private collection.)

The portraits on the following pages are from the family's private collection.

The Ninth Generation: Edmund Michael Van Buskirk (1875-1950)

Portrait 5. Edmund⁹ Michael Van Buskirk, at right, and his brother, Otis⁹ Walter Van Buskirk, at left, probably photographed for High School in Monroeville, Indiana. Edmund⁹ Michael became a physician in Fort Wayne; Otis⁹ farmed near his parents in Monroeville.

Portrait 6. Edmund⁹ Michael Van Buskirk, front row, center, in Monroeville High School photograph with classmates and teacher. Labeled on back "High School."

The Van Buskirks of Indiana

Portrait 7. Top left: Capt. Edmund⁹ Michael Van Buskirk, MD, during World War I, as photographed when he was stationed in Alabama.

Portrait 8. Top right: Edmund⁹ Michael Van Buskirk, MD, as a young physician in Fort Wayne, Indiana, and district representative for the Indiana State Medical Society.

Portrait 9. Left: Edmund⁹ Michael Van Buskirk, MD (1875–1950). Presidential photograph for Indiana State Medical Society, 1938.

CHAPTER 12

THE TENTH GENERATION: EDMUND LINFORD VAN BUSKIRK

(1907–1995)

Edmund[10] Linford Van Buskirk was born October 15, 1907 in Fort Wayne, Indiana, the tenth generation of Van Buskirks previously discussed. Edmund[10] Linford was much more to me than just my father: he was also my friend, advisor, mentor, and, eventually, colleague. Although he held himself to the highest of moral and ethical standards, my dad was never prudish, pedantic, or even severe or particularly stern. He was, instead, remarkably cognizant and tolerant of human frailties and foibles, a tolerance perhaps fueled by his medical training in rough places and tough times during the Great Depression in Indianapolis. Clearly, I was destined to follow his professional footsteps, but the granite constant of my life with him was the absolute certainty that he would support, even applaud, whatever path I chose to follow, whatever steps it to took to fulfill my aspirations. Most of his friends and colleagues called him Van, a few, "Ed." He signed documents as "E. L." but his patients and coworkers simply called him "Dr. Van." My favorites were the solicitations addressed to "Elvan Buskirk!"

My father graduated from Albion College in 1929 in Michigan where he met a young woman, named Dorothy Elizabeth Deming, from Jackson, Michigan, whom he married on Jan 30, 1930. While the young couple struggled through the Great Depression, he graduated from Indiana University Medical

School in 1933. He finished his ophthalmology and otolaryngology residency training at the same institution, in the university hospital in 1936. Although my dad loved "doctoring" in the most general and truest sense of the word, he always considered himself primarily an ophthalmologist, but couldn't shed the ear, nose, and throat part for another twenty-five years. Just as my father had completed his first year of specialty training, the two branches of the specialties of the senses split into two entirely different fields: ophthalmology (Eye) and otolaryngology (ENT). Each would develop its own training programs and certification criteria. Most graduates of that time, including my father, practiced both fields, Eye and ENT, but generally leaned toward one or the other. I remember sitting outside his office door, waiting for him to finish his day's work, trying to shut out the noxious sounds of sucking secretions, blowing sprays, and hacking coughs wafting through the door.

During World War II, he was one of the only oculo-facial surgeons left in northern Indiana, and thus, he was declared an "essential civilian." He continued to practice Eye as well as ENT for those war years and for a few after that. Despite his preference for the eye, I recall him practicing surgery on the various bones of the ear as new microsurgical operations became available. As I grew a bit older, 12–14 years old, and began to do some research of my own at Purdue University, my father taught me how to hold and manipulate the fine instruments needed to perform delicate operations, while practicing incisions and suturing on the peel of grapes. Finally, by the 1950s, his clinic was able to hire a full-time otolaryngologist, and he could at last concentrate on his first medical love, the eye.

Eventually, I too became an ophthalmologist. Although I chose a slightly different path for my ophthalmic journey, we would often discuss cases over what would become a well-worn metaphor for the love and communication between us. When I visited in Lafayette, he liked for me to scrub-in with him in surgery. I recall one time in the late 1970s, after he had done several cataract extractions, he said to me, "You might want to sit this next one

The Tenth Generation: Edmund Linford Van Buskirk (1907–1995)

out!" I asked why and he explained he was removing a young child's tonsils! Incredulous, I wondered why, after all these years, would he be undertaking a tonsillectomy. It turned out that he had taken out the mother's tonsils as well as the grandmother's; the family would have no one else do it! Although I was privileged to study with some of the most talented and prominent eye surgeons of my time, I have always believed that I learned more about the fundamentals of eye surgery from my father than from anyone else. Those early experiences of practicing surgery on grapes and learning the proper methods to manage fine surgical instruments and techniques underpinned my own modicum of success.

My parents' first child, my oldest sister, Nancy[11] Louise, was born in Indianapolis on August 27, 1931, and my second sister, Joan[11] Elizabeth, on November 25, 1935, both at the Coleman Hospital for Women in Indianapolis while my father completed his training. I, the third child, was born in Lafayette, Indiana July 13, 1941.

At least to me, when I was a child, my dad seemed to romanticize the pastoral rural life of his grandparents and sometimes liked to describe himself as a "gentleman farmer" or farm boy. He relished talking shop with his many agrarian patients who came from their farms in the surrounding rural Indiana into Lafayette for their eye care. Having been raised comfortably in the Purdue University college town, I never understood the farming reference until I began studying our family. I then realized that my father and his uncles and aunts had all been raised on the farms in Monroeville, and that he had spent many hours with his relatives there when he had been a child and young man. His claims of being a farm boy were not so farfetched. (I also have evanescent recollections of visits to those farms from so many decades ago.) To me, my dad seemed so urbane, so imbued with all that went with being a specialist doctor, I could envision him more readily in Harley Street consulting rooms than working on a farm.

When my father finished his medical training, he eschewed the time honored young doctor's ritual of "hanging out the shingle" to begin a private practice. Rather he joined a new "group practice" in a medical clinic in Lafayette, Indiana, the Arnett-Crockett Clinic, which had multiple medical specialists among its ambitions. My father eventually would lead the Arnett Clinic, serving as president through many of its most ambitious growth periods in the 1950s and 1960s as it became the multi-specialty clinic to which Dr. Arnett aspired. Today, the Arnett Clinic is part of the Indiana University Health System.

I also remember many evenings waiting impatiently for my dad to finish the day's clinic so we could go out to dinner, while he chatted with his farmer patients about the state of their crops. Farming may have been in his blood, but medicine was more deeply engrained. In my own lifelong career in medicine, I don't believe I have ever known anyone who enjoyed caring for the sick more than he did. I even remember riding in the car with my father on weekends as he made house calls.

My dad didn't really have hobbies; he always said ophthalmology was his hobby. In those days it was a cliché for a doctor to play golf on Thursday afternoons, but he didn't like golf and kept right on at his work. He loved to do his surgery on Saturday when he had the surgery theatre pretty much to himself. By the time I was in high school, he would invite me to come into the operating room to watch. After I learned to watch the local anesthetic injections around the eye without feeling faint, I would pay close attention as he delivered the lens in cataract surgery, always saying, "There's the pearl!"

My dad loved to attend medical meetings and would take most assiduous notes. There was never any question about whether or not his "Continuing Education" credentials were up to date, even after he became old, and "re-credentialing" became required for medical licensure. He proudly displayed his "CME" certificates in the hall outside his office, but for him, education meant far more than fulfilling some arbitrary minimum requirements. Long before "continuing education" became a catch phrase for maintaining physician quality, my dad stressed to me the importance of self-education. Perhaps he thought of his own father who had taught himself Latin, Greek, classical history, and so much else, even his own medical specialty of radiology. My dad successfully urged me to develop a lifelong habit of reading at night, both professionally, but especially, for general knowledge. He stressed to me that life was a process of education, and that you spend the first half of your life preparing for the last. As a reader of Conan Doyle, he could have added the Sherlock Holmes adage that the greatest lesson would be saved for the last.[Doy]

It was not surprising that my dad undertook medicine. His father was a physician, a radiologist who had started as a general doctor; many of his parent's friends were physicians. In addition, his father's two uncles, Joseph[8] Van Buskirk and A.E.[8r] Van Buskirk, were also physicians; A.E.[8r], on the faculty of the local medical college had actually taught surgical anatomy to my dad's own father, Edmund[9] Michael Van Buskirk. Then, there was Anne Elizabeth (Cree) Van Buskirk, that old pioneer "root doctor" in Ohio, making my father the third, if not fourth generation physician.

I have always felt that what made my father a great physician, more than the upbringing among physicians, were the inherent characteristics of his persona, his kindness, generosity, and undying compassionate curiosity about his fellow man. I recall one day shortly after my marriage, when my Dad was proudly showing our Indiana town of Lafayette to my newlywed wife, Bette. He took us into the local bank to introduce us to an old family friend who happened to be the bank president. As we were leaving the bank, a homeless man, lying in the gutter along the sidewalk, suddenly sat up and called "Dr. Van, Dr. Van!" My dad stopped, spoke to the man, asked him how he was doing. He introduced us to him with the same friendly dignity as he had just done moments before to the bank president. I asked my dad who the man was, and he replied that he was just a long time patient of his. I ask if the man were an alcoholic, and my dad replied, "Oh, no; he just drinks too much!"

When my father died on April 29, 1995, people of all walks of life, from all over Indiana and beyond, stood in the rain in line for hours outside the packed funeral home, waiting their turn to pay last respects to Dr. Van. It was more than final homage to a close friend, a physician with an open heart, and a great man: in many ways, they seemed to know they were paying their final tribute to one of the last great physicians of an era so rapidly dissipating into the past (see portraits 10–13).

The following portraits are from the family's private collection.

Portrait 10. Edmund[10] Linford Van Buskirk, age 4–5, with his mother, Mary Louise (Schwarze) Van Buskirk, and his baby sister, Alice Louise. Photographed ca. 1912.

Portrait 11. Edmund[10] Linford Van Buskirk as a young man in the late 1920s.

The Tenth Generation: Edmund Linford Van Buskirk (1907–1995)

Portrait 12. *Edmund¹⁰ Linford Van Buskirk, MD, in a photo taken around 1960.*

Portrait 13. *Edmund¹⁰ Linford Van Buskirk, MD, 1907–1995.*

Figure 24. Descendants of Edmund[10] Linford and Dorothy Elizabeth Van Buskirk.

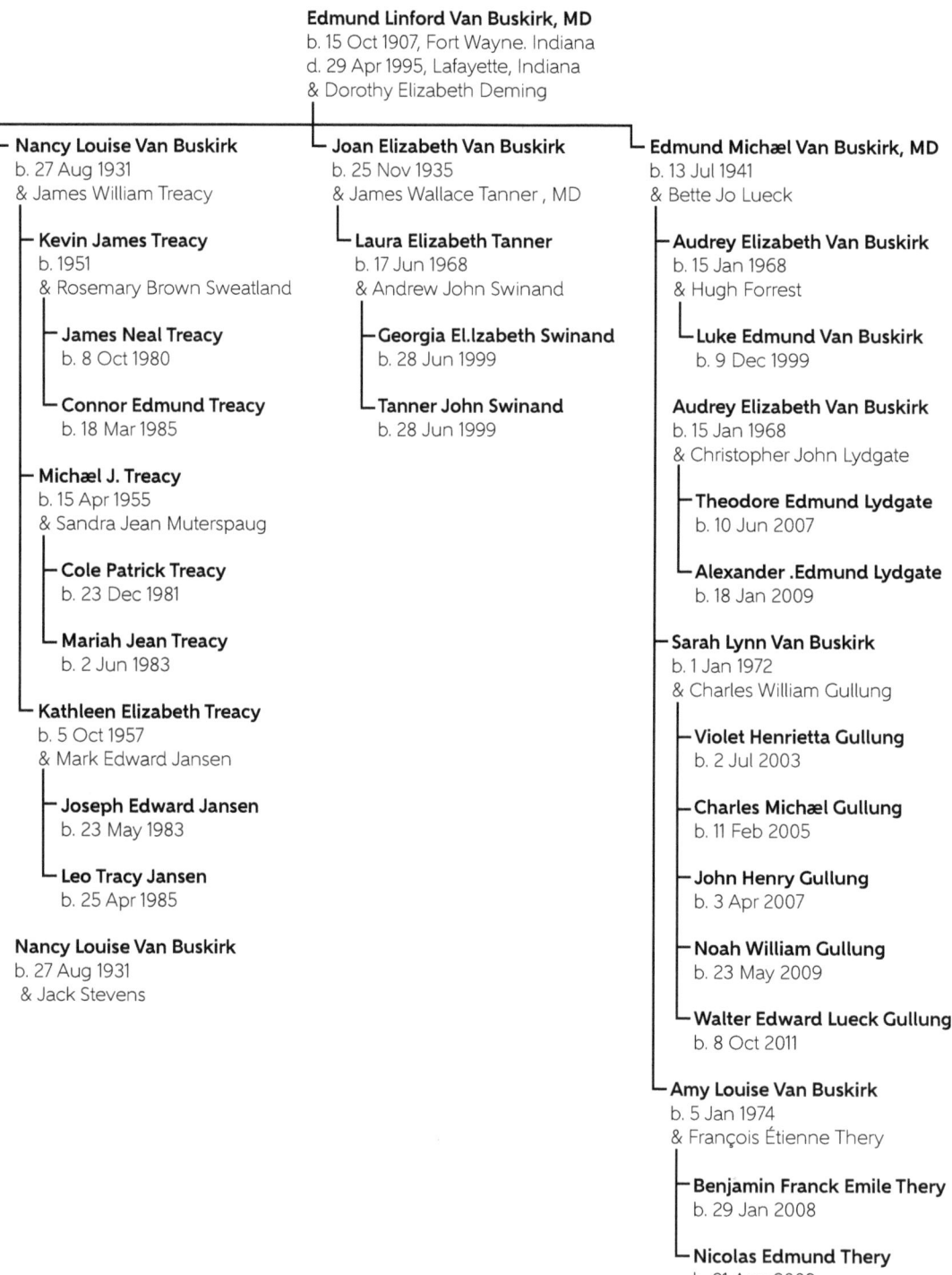

CHAPTER 13

THE BY-WAYS OF DISTANT COUSINS, I

The Loyalists

As American school children, we learn quite a bit about the American Revolution, about the colonial patriots who revolted against the tyranny of England and carved a new nation from the original thirteen British colonies. To understand fully the social climate of the time it may be useful to confront the consideration that our revolution was by no means universally embraced by all of the colonialists. At least one-sixth of them chose, at their peril, to side with the King of England. Moreover, in the New York/New Jersey regions of Van Buskirk ancestors, the percentage of Loyalists or "Tories" was far higher, even a majority. Many Loyalists joined British regiments. Others escaped to Canada, and still others were captured, tarred-and-feathered, tortured, or killed by the patriots. Thus, just as with the Civil War of the century to follow, the American Revolutionary War sometimes pitted brother against brother, son against father.

The Van Buskirks were, by no means, exempt. Perhaps they were made more susceptible to the dilemma by virtue of living in an area where the Loyalists constituted a majority. Conversely, many of the Van Buskirks who trace their direct lineage through John³ Van Buskirk, who settled in Buck's County, Pennsylvania, have discovered that they qualify as Sons or Daughters of the American Revolution. I have cited numerous examples in the preceding chapters, but we also find that just as many, probably more, Van Buskirks were Loyalists. Still others avoided the conflict altogether as pacifist Quakers.

I have presented in some detail the specific direct line of descent from Laurens[1] Andriessen Van Buskirk's eldest son, Andries[2] and his fourth son, Jan[3] (John), who had moved from Pennsylvania in the early eighteenth century. John[3] Van Buskirk died long before the hostilities began, but his son George[4] and George's[4] five sons all served in the colonial militias for the Revolutionary War. From three centuries hence, we should keep in mind that, by the time of the revolution, the majority of the sons of Andries[2] had already immigrated to Pennsylvania where they, with the majority of colonists, sided with the rebels. On the other hand, the offspring of the three younger sons of Laurens[1] Andriessen, Laurens[2], Pieter[2], and Thomas[2], for the most part, remained in the British stronghold of New York and New Jersey where the majority remained loyal to the King. Perhaps theirs was the more conflicted decision. In his essay "How George Washington Saved the Life of Abraham Van Buskirk's Son," Todd Braisted notes that the Van Buskirk family in New York was known for its strong Loyalist ties with no fewer than sixteen of them volunteering for the British Army.[B]

It may be recalled from earlier chapters that for many years, Andries[2] resided along side his younger brother, Laurens[2] Van Buskirk, at Saddle River, New Jersey. Both, of course, died long before the revolution began, but the family of Laurens[2] Van Buskirk in the Hackensack/Saddle River region of northern Bergen County particularly exemplifies the dilemma of conflicted interfamilial political loyalty. As so aptly submitted by Lorenzo Sabine in his Biographical Sketches of Loyalists of the American Revolution, the inevitable choice to join either side produced instant enemies within family, among friends and neighbors.[Sa]

Laurens[2] and Hendrickje (Van der Linde) Van Buskirk had seven sons and two daughters. The oldest three sons, Joost[3L], Andrew[3L], and Jan (John[3L]) all sided with the colonial patriots, survived the war, and lived out their lives in the states of New York or New Jersey. John[3L] Van Buskirk's devotion to the patriots was so strong that he disowned the children of his third wife, Theodosa, because they had become Loyalists.

Conversely, despite John's[3L] intense allegiance to the colonialist cause, his eldest son, Laurens[4L] Jansen Van Buskirk, became an equally avid Loyalist and evacuated to Canada with most of his family. His two married daughters, however, remained behind with their husbands; his son Abraham[5L] left with the family for Canada but returned to the United States after the war. After settling in Nova Scotia with the remaining family, their father, Laurens[4L] Jansen, disowned his children who were not with him in Canada.

Laurens's[2] fourth son, Benjamin[3L], died well before the revolution in 1762. The fifth son, Laurens[3L] Van Buskirk, lived not far from his family home in Saddle River just across the northeast border of New Jersey in a small village of Ramapos, New York where he had a small mill. Laurens[3L] Van Buskirk was widely known as the "The Miller of Ramapos." In contrast to his older brothers, he was an unequivocal Loyalist, having signed a declaration of loyalty to the English King. For his kindness to the British, "The Miller of Ramapos" was "invited" by his neighbors to leave the village and was told that if he ever returned, he would be shot on sight. He retreated with his family to outer Long Island to wait out the war. Eventually, they were evacuated to New Brunswick and Nova Scotia where Laurens[3L] served as colonel in the British Colonial Army in Canada. Ultimately, Laurens[3L], "The Miller of Ramapos," settled in Nova Scotia where he lived out his life. Just within this small family branch, the revolution had turned brother against brother, son against father.

Pieter[2] Van Buskirk, the third son of Laurens[1], had five sons and seven daughters. Pieter's[2] youngest son, Abraham died young. Similarly, his eldest son, Laurens[3] Pietersen Van Buskirk, had two sons, Lawrence[4], who died at age 17, and Pieter[4], who married Catherine Hanse Van Barkeloo and does appear to have been a Loyalist. Of all Pieter's[2] grandsons, the names only of the two sons of his fourth son, Jacobus[3] Pietersen Van Buskirk, Peter[4] and John[4], are mentioned in regard to the Tories. On July 8, 1776, both Peter[4] and John[4] were accused of communicating with enemy (i.e., colluding with the British), but they were both tried and acquitted. Both lived out their lives on or near the family farms at Constable Hook.

On the other hand, British Colonel Abraham[4L] Van Buskirk, the grandson of Laurens's[1] fourth son, Thomas[2], became perhaps the most prominent of the Van Buskirk Loyalists. Thomas[2] Van Buskirk's son, Jacobus[3], whose wife is unknown, had four sons, two of whom were Loyalists. Abraham[4L] Van Buskirk had been a prominent physician, surgeon, and apothecary in Teaneck, New Jersey, and a member of the Provincial Congress. He and many of the other "Dutch" colonists had pressed hard for moderation and a diplomatic negotiation with the British, but the tide in Bergen County gradually turned in favor of rebellion. Most of his friends and neighbors knew of Abraham's[4]—and most of his family's—preference to remain with the British. Even as the specter of war loomed, Van Buskirk was elected as a moderate to the Provincial Congress, and he became an officer in the Bergen County Militia. However, he ultimately would not renounce his allegiance to the Crown and subsequently resigned from the Provincial Congress. On November 22, 1776, the British Army crossed the Hackensack River into Bergen County. As the residents quickly aligned themselves with one side or the other, Abraham[4L] Van Buskirk assembled his Volunteer Loyalists who now declared their allegiance to the Crown and formed the 3rd Battalion of New Jersey Volunteers, a British unit known as "Skinner's Greens." He was immediately appointed to lieutenant colonel. He distinguished himself in numerous battles in the early years of the war and also served as surgeon to his unit.[S] Abraham[4L] had entered the British Army service with the understanding that his 16-year-old son, Jacob[5L], would join him. On January 17, 1777. Jacob[5L] was appointed lieutenant but was soon promoted to captain.

Remarkably, the British Captain Jacob[5L] owed his life to General George Washington. During a diversionary patriot excursion onto Staten Island directed by Major General Philemon Dickinson, senior officer of the New Jersey Militia, Captain Jacob[5L] Van Buskirk was captured with two other officers while they were sleeping in a boarding house. The three men were taken by the colonial militia, imprisoned, and condemned to hanging by the local officials. However, before hanging three British officers, Major General Dickinson thought it best to clear the proceedings with General Washington, who forbad the hanging. Washington explained that those soldiers had been free to make their own choice to side with the British. Thus, much to the consternation of Major General Dickinson, George Washington spared Captain Van Buskirk and the two other officers. The Van Buskirk family ultimately evacuated to Nova Scotia where they became prominent Canadian citizens. After the war, they moved to Shelburne, Nova Scotia, where Colonel Abraham[4L] Van Buskirk served as Mayor.[B]

In a similar vein of Washington's humanity, during the early stages of the war, Colonel Abraham's[4L] wife and younger children had been evacuated from Hackensack to one of the Van Buskirk farms on Constable Hook. She had written to her husband, describing their hardships when General Washington's troops landed at Van Buskirk Point and were encamped upon their land (see fig. 6). The rebel troops had overrun their crops and stolen their cows, leaving Mrs. Van Buskirk without sustenance for the family. In these dire straights, she appealed for help directly to General Washington, whom she described as a fine gentleman. Despite the well-known Loyalist leanings of these Van Buskirks, Washington ordered his troops to leave their farm and possessions alone. Further, he went so far as to post a corporal with a guard of soldiers for the family's protection, though he also strongly advised that the Van Buskirk family should evacuate to a safer place as soon as possible.[S,Sa]

In addition, the colonel's older brother, Lawrence[4L] Jacobus Van Buskirk, and his four sons also were Loyalists. Their father, James[3L] Van Buskirk, was born in 1704, was over 70 at the time of the independence, but lived throughout his life at Hackensack, presumably loyal to the rebel patriots. Although his sons—

Colonel Abraham[4L] and Lawrence[4L] Jacobus (a captain in the King's Orange Rangers)—were both Loyalists, their brother James[4L] was a "Violent Rebel." Three of Lawrence[4L] Jacobus's sons were officers in British regiments; his fourth son died at sea on a British privateer. As the war ended, James[4L] absconded with his privateer nephew's portion of his father's estate by threatening Lawrence[4L] Jacobus that unless he turned over the land, all of his property would be seized by the Americans and handed over to him (James[4L]).[S]

If I have included perhaps tedious detail about these mixed loyalties of the children of Laurens[2], Pieter[2], and Thomas[2] Van Buskirk, it has only been to underscore the personal familial tragedy inflicted by the war on both sides. It was among these branches that the disagreements were most blatant, but the others were not entirely exempt. It likewise seems important to emphasize that although many of the Van Buskirks achieved success in the newly formed United States, those who chose Canada also prospered socially and politically, contributing to the development of that nation.

CHAPTER 14

WESTERN MIGRATION

The Final Leg on the Oregon Trail

WHEN MY FAMILY AND I closed the door on our Rexmont, Pennsylvania house in June of 1979, we gave no thought to our progenitors who had similarly left their homes in Pennsylvania at the end of the eighteenth century to seek new opportunities in the West. In fact, our embarkation along the Pennsylvania Turnpike approximated the old Lancaster Road by which they traveled from Philadelphia through Lancaster as far as the Susquehanna River. By the same token, as we continued our travels over the Great American Plains and western mountains to the Willamette River Valley of Oregon, we gave little consideration to my father's offhand comment that Van Buskirks had crossed the plains on the Oregon Trail. We drove our comfortable sedan over sleek interstate highways, oblivious to the fact that our wheels were roughly tracing the far more arduous ventures of our distant relatives nearly 130 years earlier. We glided along at a mile per minute, not at less than one mile per hour in choking dust over rutted tracks among throngs of wagons, bumping ox nose to wagon tail. Our cross-country journey lasted a few days; theirs, six months from the banks of the Missouri to the Pacific Northwest.

The musty documents of the past provide virtually no insight into the specific motivations for the peoples' deeds that they record, but it is not difficult to postulate what these pioneering Van Buskirks must have had in mind. They were but one family in a migration of nearly a half-million people who undertook the arduous and heartbreaking 2,000-mile western trek between 1840 and 1865. There was the current of excitement for what we now refer to as "Manifest Destiny," a term coined by a newspaper editor, John O'Sullivan, in 1845. The conviction, if not the term, had been expressed for decades; before that it was the destiny of the United States to settle from coast to coast, from Canada to Mexico. As a practical matter, in the years following Lewis and Clark's Corps of Discovery mission, the United States government had been encouraging settlers to establish themselves in the Oregon Territory. There seemed to have been a sense that an American presence in the Pacific Northwest might be sufficient to discourage British southern territorial expansion from western Canada into the Oregon Territory. Of course, by 1849, it was gold that drew people to California, but that was an entirely different story. Nonetheless, for the first half of the trip, the gold rush "forty-niners" and the Oregon pioneers followed the same trail for a thousand miles until it branched at Fort Bridges or Fort Hall southward through Utah to the California gold fields or northward to Oregon.

The pioneers on the Oregon Trail invariably used oxen, yoked in a pair to pull their wagons. The oxen were strong: they could travel great distances and could subsist on a wide variety of vegetation. Because the Conestoga wagons of the pioneer predecessors in the East were much too big and heavy for the Oregon Trail, they typically adapted a farm wagon with a bed that was 4 feet wide and 10–11 feet long, a foot or so in depth. The width of the iron-tired wheels was crucial because if they were too narrow, the wheels would sink into the desert sand, yet moderately narrow worked best on the hard surfaces of the rocky trails elsewhere. In addition, they used much heavier axles than were needed on the farm because a broken axle would be disastrous in the western wilderness, compelling them either to convert the wagon to an awkward two-wheeler or abandon it with all but what they could carry.[Tr]

Western Migration: The Final Leg on the Oregon Trail

Around mid-April each year, Oregon Trail pioneers began to assemble along the Missouri River, where they would begin their trek. Many came up the river by boat from St Louis and would encamp near Independence, St. Joseph, or one of the other "jumping off" places. By the end of the month, these locations would become extremely crowded with thousands of pioneers waiting for nature's signs to go. Then, they would wait again to board their wagons onto the limited ferries in order to cross the river. One man, who had arrived late to the embarkation point, recorded that it took him four days of searching to find his family among the throngs in line for the ferry. By 1850, it typically took around five to six months to cover 2,100 miles along the Trail to Oregon. The group couldn't leave until sufficient grass had grown along the way to feed their animals, but they knew they mustn't delay beyond that because they had to cross the Blue Mountains and descend to the Columbia and Willamette valleys before the hard snows of early winter started. Thus, they had a window of only a few weeks through which to begin their journey if they were to reach their destination successfully. The infamous Donner party who died in the Sierra Nevada mountain range had been delayed by flooding of the rivers in Kansas in 1846. It had held them up sufficiently for them to become trapped months later in a blinding blizzard in the western mountains. The rule of thumb was to wait until the prairie grass was four inches tall to assure sufficient animal feed, and then start promptly.[Tr]

Of course, the families had packed all of their most prized possessions that they thought the wagons could haul, as well as about a ton of supplies and provisions for a family of four. The supplies mainly consisted of food staples: flour, sugar, coffee, and bacon. The coffee would be used to mask the foul taste of the stagnant water they would have to drink, and the bacon would be the best preserved of available meats, though they planned to shoot some game along the way. They loaded their wagons to the brim with the supplies and goods, leaving no room for passengers. All but the smallest toddlers and the most infirm walked along side the wagons the entire way to Oregon. Even so, in the first few days, most realized that the wagons were vastly overloaded, and they began to jettison those once prized, but now superfluous, possessions along the trail that soon became festooned with fine furniture, trunks, even cast iron stoves, discarding these last vestiges of the civilization that they were leaving behind.

In general, parties on the Oregon Trail managed an average of 15 miles per day, and spent about twelve hours on the trail. After a few days, most established a fairly rigid routine. They would arise before sunup, around 5:00 a.m., prepare the wagons and oxen teams, cook the breakfast, and be on the trail by 6:00 a.m. Generally, they would stop for lunch and again for the night well before dark, around 6:00 p.m. The travelers normally would bed down by nightfall around 9:00 p.m. Most slept in the open. They did indeed circle their wagons at night—not as a defensive maneuver against attack, but rather to form a kind of corral to contain their livestock.[Tr]

River crossings were always challenging. In some cases the pioneers would convert their wagon box into a makeshift boat by caulking the joints and removing the wheels. As the trek became more popular, entrepreneurial ferryman would spring up along the rivers often charging exorbitant rates. To cross the fast-moving Kansas River, the ferry charged $4, about $120 in today's currency. One enterprising ferryman who plied the rough and dangerous Green River in Northwest Wyoming managed to collect $65,000 in single summer, approximating a dollar value in 2017 of nearly $2 million!

As the pioneers proceeded overland, steep inclines and precipitous descents posed recurring, horrendous challenges and risks. One of the most dangerous was the Big Hill descent in Eastern Idaho. There, the men would all pull heavy rope lines tied to the rear of the wagon to slow its descent, but the site nonetheless caused many disastrous crashes of runaway wagons.

Perhaps the most horrific irony was that when they finally reached the banks of the Columbia, exhausted but relieved to have made it over the Blue Mountains before the winter snowfall, the pioneers faced what would prove to be one final supreme test of their mettle. Just 100 miles from the Willamette Valley, the way westward was blocked by a giant obstacle in the form of Mount Hood. Prior to 1846, the pioneers had to take to the raging Columbia River to make their way to the Willamette. At first, they would sell their teams, wagons, and other heavy items and hire local Indians to navigate them downriver through the dangerous rapids. Later, access to ferries became available but, as at the Kansas River, the costs were exorbitant. However, in 1846, Sam Barlow completed a new trail, the Barlow Road, that ran from The Dalles, Oregon, on the Columbia River around the southern part of Mount Hood to Oregon City on the Willamette River, approximating today's US Highway 26. The tremendous inclines and descents made the crossing one of the most arduous and perilous, but it brought the Oregon Trail pioneers finally to their destination without the perils of the raging Columbia.

CHAPTER 15

THE BY-WAYS OF DISTANT COUSINS, II

Van Buskirks on the Oregon Trail

After four or five days of easy, if tedious, driving, my family and I arrived in Oregon from Pennsylvania in 1979. I needed another four decades to work out the details of my father's casual remark about the Van Buskirks on the Oregon Trail. It went like this: George[4] Van Buskirk's firstborn son, older brother to my direct ancestor, Joseph[5], was the capricious John[5] Van Buskirk who had enlisted in a different Revolutionary War Northampton Pennsylvania battalion than his father and brothers. He departed for western Maryland before the war ended. John[5] and his wife, Mary, had eight children: seven sons and one daughter. As I was able to divine from John[5] Van Buskirk's family bible, two of his sons, Joseph[6b] and Andrew, died in infancy. As noted, John[5] and Mary had moved to the Linton Hundred, Maryland, just as the Revolutionary War was drawing to a close. Perhaps that war had contributed to his seemingly mercurial nature. He banished another of his sons from his home because of "liquor." The young man also went west, never to be heard from again. John[5] Van Buskirk seemed to be closest to his youngest son, William[6ot], who witnessed his will and served as executor.

William[6ot] Van Buskirk was born in Linton Hundred, Maryland, on June 6, 1789. Like his brothers and many of his cousins, on reaching maturity, William[6ot] migrated west, in his case to Kentucky, sometime after 1810. There, he taught school in 1815, and he met Margaret Evans whom he married. His brother George[6], twenty-one years his senior, had married Mary Rulon before 1800, also had moved to Kentucky, but eventually moved to Wayne County, Indiana, on the Ohio border. William[6ot] and Margaret moved from Kentucky to Knox County, in central Ohio where, like their cousins to the east in the Tuscarawas valley, they carved out a farm from the dense virgin forest.

For reasons not specifically clear but likely no different from many other pioneers, as detailed in the previous chapter, the William[6ot] Van Buskirks decided at mid-century to join the great migration west, along the Oregon Trail to the Pacific Northwest. The most specific incentive, likely the key factor for the William[6ot] Van Buskirk family, was the Oregon Land Donation Act of 1850. That act provided free land to American settlers who would establish permanent residence in Oregon—320 acres to any individual or 640 acres for a family. The fervor reached its peak in 1852, the year of the Van Buskirk's trek when they joined some 70,000 fellow migrants. In addition, the more mundane matters of climate and disease undoubtedly weighed heavily on their minds as well. The fierce midwestern winters followed by the terrible pestilence of malaria and yellow fever that the warm weather brought along the marshy riverbanks each summer contrasted unfavorably with tales of mild winters and verdant fertile valleys of Oregon.

The entire William[6ot] Van Buskirk family with their six children, two sons-in-law, two daughters-in-law and eleven grandchildren struck out on October 2, 1851. Fortunately for us, their 24-year-old son, Andrew[7ot], kept a fairly regular, if terse, journal that preserves remarkable details about the yearlong trek. He reports not only about the well-known landmarks, but especially about their relationships and hardships along the way, including the sad reports of the terrible sickness and death that afflicted them. Merrill J. Mattes collected and published excerpts of some 2,000 such narratives, with commentary, in 1988.[Ma] He noted that Andrew Van Buskirk's was one of the shortest and least detailed of the journals that he reviewed, but today's reader will be struck by the evocative and unvarnished descriptions of familial squabbles and cooperation along the route.[Ma] To my view, Andrew[7ot] provides unusually poignant insight from a young man into the suffering and tragic deaths of his mother and five other close relatives (see fig. 25). I have reproduced the typescript of the entire journal in the appendix.

After crossing the Indiana border, William's[6ot] family stayed for a night with their "cousins" at William Van Buskirk's farm. It is not clear exactly who these William Van Buskirk cousins were, but were almost certainly one of two families with farms along their route in eastern Indiana. As mentioned above, William's[6ot] older brother George[6] (Andrew's[7ot] uncle) and his wife, Mary

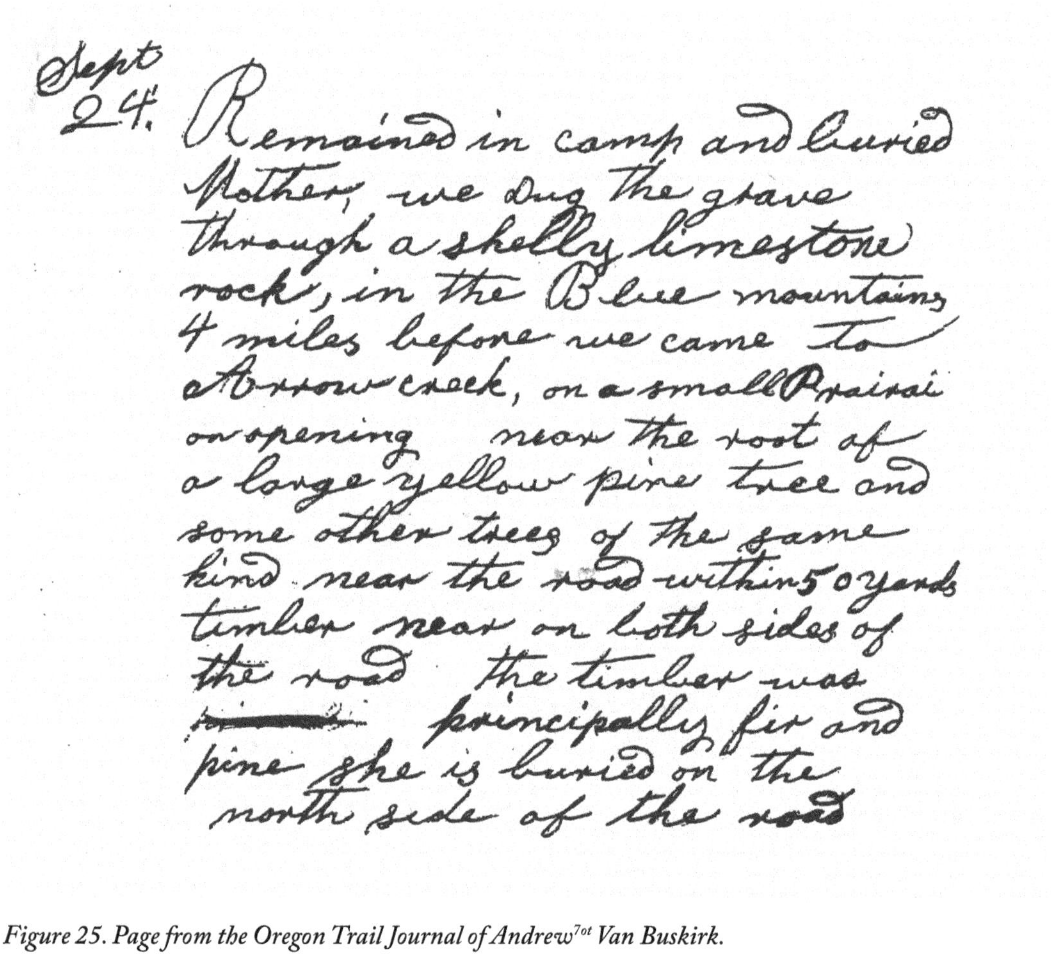

Sept 24. Remained in camp and buried Mother, we dug the grave through a shelly limestone rock, in the Blue mountains 4 miles before we came to Arrow creek, on a small Prairai or opening near the root of a large yellow pine tree and some other trees of the same kind near the road within 50 yards timber near on both sides of the road the timber was principally fir and pine she is buried on the north side of the road

Figure 25. Page from the Oregon Trail Journal of Andrew[7ot] Van Buskirk.

(Rulon), had moved from Pennsylvania to Estill, Kentucky and then to Wayne County, Indiana. George[6] died in 1829, but he had at least two sons living in the area. His son William[7] and Mary Van Buskirk had a farm, likely inherited from his father in Wayne County, near Milton, Indiana, just west of Richmond. By the same token, William's[7] brother John[7] and John's wife, Dulcena (Huff) Van Buskirk, farmed in Henry County, Indiana, just east of Indianapolis, and their son William[8] was, indeed, Andrew's[7ot] cousin. Both of these farms were along the Van Buskirk's route across Indiana.

After leaving their Indiana cousin's farm, the William[6ot] Van Buskirk party moved directly east, approximating what eventually became US Highway 36. They crossed into the state of Illinois, finally reaching the Mississippi River. They camped for the night on the eastern bank of the river and then ferried across at Hannibal, Missouri, on October 26, 1851. Over the next week or so they crossed through the Territory of Missouri, through Chilicothe, then Gallatin, then Rochester, and finally to "the Van Buskirk Settlement," an encampment just east of the Missouri River. There they remained for the winter of 1851–1852, wisely not wanting to undertake the Oregon Trail in winter.

The decision to go as far as the Missouri River in the autumn and then wait until spring to embark upon the great trek across the plain was an intelligent one, undoubtedly influenced by stories of the many who had preceded them on the Trail. It was the standard and safest approach because they only had about a two-week window in May in which they could start and still make Oregon without becoming snowbound in the western mountains.

On April 29, 1852, the Van Buskirks renewed their trek, crossing the Missouri River at Elizabethtown, about a mile north of Amazonia, Missouri, not far from the popular crossing spot at St. Joseph. From Andrew's[7ot] journal, it seems that Elizabethtown was a fairly common crossing site and setting off place for Oregon Trail travelers who could make use of the general supply store there that was operated by E.H. Perry and Young. Oddly, of the 2,000 Oregon Trail narratives compiled by Mattes, only Andrew's[7ot] journal mentioned the little town. Mattes further states, incorrectly, that Elizabethtown is "now unidentifiable."[Ma] The site of Elizabethtown, one mile north of the present day Amazonia on the Missouri River is, in fact, well documented, down to the above mentioned general store and even the availability of a wagon train bound for California supervised by Elias H. Perry departing in the same year, 1852.[Da] Thus, from Elizabethtown, Missouri, they embarked, heading due west, across Kansas to the Blue River, then north to reach the true Oregon Trail in Nebraska.

Since they crossed the Missouri River near St. Joseph at Elizabethtown, the Van Buskirk party likely followed the St. Joseph jumping off place on the St. Joseph trail, first blazed in 1844 by Cornelius Gilliam to merge with the main trail from Independence.[Ba] As the trek west became more and more crowded with each passing year, emigrants began to seek jumping off places other than Independence along the Missouri River, and St. Joseph became another popular one. Going slightly out of the way to the now obscure Elizabethtown probably saved the Van Buskirk party much precious time. It was not unusual for the emigrants to have to wait several weeks for a ferry at major crossing points that were camped with the wagons hub-to-hub over areas as large as three square miles. As mentioned earlier, sometimes in desperation, they would remove the wheels and axles from the wagon, caulk the joints, and float across the river in a sort of makeshift box shaped boat or barge.

Once across the Missouri River, in what is now Donophan County, Kansas, it would have taken them about a week or so traveling west to reach the ford over the Wolf River, where they camped around May 13, 1852. On that date, Andrew[7ot] finally had an opportunity to make his first journal entries after leaving Missouri. It was in this journal entry that he describes the chaos induced by the many wagons converging, crowding, and crashing into one another. Some of the oxen teams became panicked and stampeded, fortunately without injury other than a broken yoke that the travelers were able to repair on one wagon. Andrew[7ot] also wrote about crossing the Blue River, some 75 miles further west, near the present day town of Marysville, Kansas. This area was the first of the sort of oases that the travelers would occasionally encounter, rich with green foliage and fresh water nearby at Alcove Springs. Alcove Springs became a welcome first layover stop for the emigrants. Exhausted by the early stages of their trek and daunted by the hardships that inevitably lay ahead, some of them abandoned their plans and settled there in central Kansas.

But the Van Buskirk party moved on, traveling north along the banks of Blue River until they encountered the bluffs of Platte River. At this point, toward the end of May, Andrew[7ot] begins to describe the terrible episodes of dysentery that would eventually sicken them all and take six of their lives. It was also at this point that they had merged with other wagon trains from the other jumping off places to join the main stream of wagon teams headed west on the Oregon Trail.

To say that such a trip was difficult, daunting, and arduous vastly understates the situation. The trail was racked with pestilence, disease, and hazards from mud, sand, and landslides, on top of fear of Indian attacks. Families typically traveled in large groups, as did the Van Buskirks. By mid-May they encountered tales of an Indian having been shot, and they were on their guard, but the journal does not report any first-hand adverse encounters. This should not be surprising because Indian attacks were actually quite uncommon until the waning years of the wagon trains during the 1860s.

Andrew[7ot] does not tell us the specific number of wagons in their group, but he describes the road as crowded with wagons as they embarked. He reports intense confusion and quarreling among the various parties throughout the first two weeks, but these issues soon became minor as they learned to cope with day-to-day challenges for survival. He frequently mentions the Whisler wagon (his sister Sarah[7ot] and her husband, Elijah Whisler) running ahead or behind them. They seemed to have quarreled for most of the trip with the Whislers, who left the group entirely on one occasion, but they seem to have reunited later.

Although the 1851 autumnal portion of the trip from Ohio to western Missouri apparently passed fairly uneventfully, the real challenges began once they embarked upon the actual Oregon Trail. The wagon teams became frightened and stampeded a few times but to no ill effect. Some emigrants were injured or even killed in such wagon accidents but a far greater risk were the infectious diseases that killed some 10 percent of the travelers on the Oregon Trail. The Van Buskirk toll was more than double that, almost 25 percent. The trailside was littered with shallow graves of the pioneer predecessors whose grief stricken relatives knew they must bury their dead and quickly move on to reach Oregon before winter snows covered the eastern Oregon mountains. Many of the graves were disrupted by scavenging animals with human skeletal fragments lying out in the open.

The deaths were primarily caused by intestinal infections contracted by consuming contaminated food and water infested with such agents as salmonella, shigella, or cholera. Understanding of microbial infection, germs, and hygiene would have to wait a few decades, but if they had just known to boil their water, many would have been saved. Cholera was particularly virulent and would kill the weakened travelers sometimes within hours of them first feeling unwell. And fresh water was hard to come by, especially in the desert of western Nebraska and Wyoming. From Andrew's[7ot] notes, I don't believe anyone in their party escaped illness, and perhaps they were lucky that only six died. Early on, Andrew[7ot], himself, became so ill he could hardly stand. He recalls going hunting but was too sick to bring the rifle to his face. Fortunately, he recovered, unlike one of the other young men, "Snyder," who was the first to die in June of 1852. They buried him near Chimney Rock in Nebraska. Then the toll of sickness really took hold over the summer. Andrew's older brother, Joseph T.[7ot] Van Buskirk, became extremely ill and died at four o'clock in the morning of August 14, 1872; his young daughter Mary[8ot] died that same afternoon. They were buried together alongside the trail.

For hundreds of miles the wagon train followed the Platte River, a wide, generally placid river only a few inches deep, rife with insects skimming across the surface, and so muddy one could hardly see the bottom of a drinking cup. Mary's[8ot] mother, Sarah[7ot] (Eldridge) Van Buskirk, died just a week later on August 20, 1852. The fifth to die on the trip was Andrew's[7ot] mother, Margaret I. (Evans) Van Buskirk, on September 23, 1852, in the Blue Mountains of eastern Oregon. It was these Blue Mountains that the pioneers needed to cross well before the winter snows and the month of October were nigh (see fig. 26). They had to dig through shale rock to prepare a suitable grave for Andrew's[7ot] mother in the mountains. Mary's sister Arminda[8ot] died a few weeks later on October 11.

Figure 26. Oregon Trail Ruts, Flagstaff Hill, Baker City, Oregon. Thousands of wheels eroded into the rock to leave their trail still visible today. Photographed by the author, May 2017.

The William[6ot] Van Buskirk family would require six months to reach their destination in the Pacific Northwest, arriving at the Willamette River at the end of October, 1852. It happened that they had picked the busiest year ever to make their trek along with the other 70,000 other emigrants. Traffic, then as now, was one the most irksome issues, especially as the multiple feeder trails coalesced onto the main route in eastern Nebraska. The wagons ran ox nose to the tail of the wagon ahead from horizon behind to the horizon ahead, barely visible in the churning dust thicker than the densest fog. Seventy-thousand neatly spaced sets of wagon wheels inexorably ground deep ruts into the underlying rock, ruts that can still be seen in places today (see fig. 27).

Elijah Whisler survived the trip and thrived for another forty years in Oregon, but his wife, Sarah[7ot] (Van Buskirk) Whistler, was so weakened that,

Figure 27. Blue Mountains of Eastern Oregon. Photographed by the author, May 2017.

Figure 28. Oregon Trail Van Buskirk gravestones, Amity Pioneer Cemetery, Amity, Oregon. Left to Right: William^{6ot} Van Buskirk, Andrew^{7ot} Van Buskirk, John^{7ot} Van Buskirk, John's wife, Sarah Sloane (Henderson) Van Buskirk, and John and Sarah's son, Lafayette^{8ot} Van Buskirk. The lighter gray monument in the center is not a Van Buskirk. Photographed by the author, May 2017.

although she completed the trek, she did not live through the winter, dying on February 11, 1853 in Amity, Oregon. Andrew^{7ot}, his brother John^{7ot}, and his father, William^{6ot}, (see portrait 14) survived the trip and established farms in Oregon. William^{6ot} died in 1859, Andrew^{7ot} in 1877. They are buried in Amity (see fig. 28).

The full text of Andrew^{7ot} Van Buskirk's *Diary of the Oregon Trail* appears in the Appendix.

The Van Buskirks of Indiana

Figure 29. Edited Genealogical Chart showing George⁴ Van Buskirk as our common ancestor with the William Van Buskirk family on the Oregon Trail.

- **George Van Buskirk**
  b. 1721, Manor of Moreland, Pennsylvania
  d. 30 Mar 1800, Chestnuthill, Northampton Co, Pennsylvania
  & Sarah ? Ashton

  - **John Van Buskirk**
    b. 1745
    d. 1829
    & Marie Blackmore

    - **George Van Buskirk**
      b. 1767
      & Mary Rulon

      - **John Van Buskirk**
        b. 1789
        d. 1859
        & Dulcena Huff

    - **William Van Buskirk**
      b. 6 Jun 1789, Washington Co Maryland
      d. 9 Oct 1859, Yamhill, Oregon
      & Margaret I Evans

      - **Sarah Van Buskirk**
        d. 11 Feb 1853

      - **John Van Buskirk**
        b. 9 Sep 1818, Knox Co, Ohio
        d. 27 Oct 1874, Yamhill Co, Oregon
        & Sarah Henderson

        - **William Van Buskirk**
          b. 1822
          d. 4 Aug 1830, Knox Co, Ohio

        - **Joseph T. Van Buskirk**
          b. 8 Oct 1824, Ohio
          & Sarah Eldridge

        - **Andrew Van Buskirk**
          b. 19 Dec 1827, Knox Co, Ohio
          d. 29 Oct 1877, Yamhill Co, Oregon

        - **Daniel Van Buskirk**
          b. 29 Aug 1833, Ohio
          d. 1900, Oregon

  - **Joseph Van Buskirk**
    b. 1751, Bucks Co, Pennsylvania
    d. 31 May 1821, Hamilton Twp, Northampton Co, Pa
    & Mary Strawn

    - **Joseph Van Buskirk**
      b. 20 Apr 1782, Hamilton Twp, Monroe Co, Pa
      d. 30 May 1864, Warwick Twp, Tuscarawas Co, Ohio
      & Rebecca Villars

      - **James Van Buskirk**
        b. 4 Sep 1811, Pennsylvania
        d. 15 Feb 1869
        & Annie Morrow

        - **Linford Van Buskirk**
          b. 4 Jul 1847, Carroll Co, Ohio
          d. 15 Oct 1910, Monroeville, Indiana
          & Mary Knouse

          - **Edmund Michæl Van Buskirk, MD**
            b. 11 Feb 1875, Monroeville, Indiana
            d. 18 Jan 1950, Fort Wayne, Indiana
            & Mary Louise Schwarze

            - **Edmund Linford Van Buskirk, MD**
              b. 15 Oct 1907, Fort Wayne, Indiana
              d. 29 Apr 1995, Lafayette, Indiana
              & Dorothy Elizabeth Deming

              - **Nancy Louise Van Buskirk**
                b. 27 Aug 1931, Indianapolis, Indiana
                & James William Treacy

              - **Joan Elizabeth Van Buskirk**
                b. 25 Nov 1935, Indianapolis, Indiana
                & James Wallace Tanner, MD

              - **Edmund Michæl Van Buskirk, MD**
                b. 13 Jul 1941, Lafayette, Indiana
                & Bette Jo Lueck

Portrait 14. William^{6ot} Van Buskirk, family leader of the trek across the plains on the Oregon Trail. His son, Andrew^{7ot} Van Buskirk, recorded the journey in his Oregon Trail Journal *(see Appendix). Photo from Joseph Gaston and George H. Himes's* The Centennial History of Oregon, *taken by unknown photographer.*[Ga]

CHAPTER 16

THE BY-WAYS OF DISTANT COUSINS, III

Captain David Van Buskirk: The Tallest Man in the Union Army

I RECALL MORE THAN ONE OCCASION from my youth when my father would remark over the dinner table that one of his patients had seen the tombstones of our "kin" down in Gosport, a small community in southern Indiana, some 20 miles north of Bloomington, Indiana. Any account of my family would somehow be incomplete without some mention of those famous Indiana Van Buskirks of Gosport, in particular Captain David Van Buskirk, "The Tallest Man in the Union Army."

The story has been told many times in feature magazine articles, scholarly historical documents, and a book entitled *Giants of the Cornfields*.[Mo] The Gosport Van Buskirks are indeed our kin, but are about as distant cousins as could possibly occur, sharing only one North American ancestor, the first, our patriarch Laurens[1] Andriessen Van Buskirk who died over three centuries ago. Nonetheless, the story is a famous one in Indiana and pervades our familial lore. The northern Indiana or "Fort Wayne Van Buskirks" are descended from Laurens[1] Andriessen's first son, Andries[2]. The Gosport Van Buskirks descend from Laurens[1] Andriessen's fourth son, Major Thomas[2]. Major Thomas[2] originally married Margritie Brickers, and after her death, he married Volkertie Collier on May 18, 1720. Major Thomas's[2] second son by his second wife was Michael[3d] Van Buskirk, born March 6, 1721. Michael[3d] married Mary Vandeventer in

1745. Michael[3d] was a Captain of the Shenandoah Revolutionary Militia during the Revolutionary War and moved to Hampshire County, Virginia in 1779. He died in Pennsylvania in 1793. He and Mary had nine children; one daughter, Mary, and eight sons, the fourth of whom was Isaac[4d], born in Louden County, Virginia on October 7, 1760.

Isaac[4d] Van Buskirk married Jerusha Little in Virginia on February 27, 1780. As with many of the other Van Buskirk family branches, Isaac[4d] and Jerusha went west after the war, through Ohio, and settled in Monroe County, Indiana in 1805. Jerusha died there on February 27, 1827, and was buried in the Van Buskirk Graveyard that still exists in Gosport under a variety of names. Isaac[4d] survived until October 27, 1843. Isaac[4d] and Jerusha had twelve children including eight sons, the seventh being James[5d] Van Buskirk who was born in Ohio on October 11, 1796. James[5d] married Maria Campbell on January 21, 1826.

James[5d] and Maria (Campbell) Van Buskirk were parents to eight children—all of whom exceeded six feet in height, but David[6d] was the tallest.

David[6d] Van Buskirk was born on November 23, 1826 in Gosport, Indiana, about 20 miles north of Bloomington, in Monroe County. The family had a farm of 450 acres of fine bottomland near the White River. His father, James[5d], at six feet one inch, was himself well above average height, and his mother's family were said to all be quite tall. By the age of 14, David[6d] was already a big young man reaching nearly 6 feet, 4 inches, though he was always a gentle man. Even as a youth, he worried that he would hurt someone if he hit too hard and was reluctant to confront others, even if provoked. On March 16, 1849, David[6d] married his first cousin Lucy Ann[6d] Van Buskirk, who grew up on an adjacent farm. Lucy's father, Isaac[5d], was James's[5d] older brother.

By the time David[6d] was 21, he had become a giant of a man, nearly 380 pounds, six feet, ten-and-one-half inches tall, by far taller than the tallest of his brothers. He was recruited by a local man Peter Kopp, himself over six feet in height, who was forming a unique Indiana regiment known as the Monroe

County Grenadiers in which sixty-one members were over six feet in height. The average Union soldier measured around five-feet-eight inches.[Mo] David's[6d] brothers Isaac[6d]—"Blue Ike"—and John[6d]—"Sandy"—joined him, as did about one hundred others. On September 12, 1861, they became Company F of the 27th Indiana Infantry and headed off to fight in the Civil War. People gathered from miles around to see David[6d] Van Buskirk and the company of "giants" march by.

The quartermaster had a devil of a time finding large enough boots for Van Buskirk and his fellow large soldiers and was forced to trade dozens of normal sized shoes to get one pair to fit his "giants!" David[6d] once wore out five horses on a twenty-four-hour forced march (see portrait 15).

Portrait 15.
Captain David[6d] Van Buskirk (1826–1886), Gosport, Indiana, the "Tallest man in the Union Army."[Du] Photo attributed to Wilbur D. Jones, Jr., Giants in the Cornfield, the 27th Indiana Infantry.[J]

Unfortunately, he was captured on May 25, 1862 and taken prisoner by the Confederates. He became quite a spectacle among the prisoners and was singled out by his captors for display wherever they went. Eventually, he was taken to Richmond where the Confederate President Jefferson Davis came to see him. David[6d] agreed to be exhibited in a hotel as a kind of freak show, in exchange for food. He was one of the few Confederate prisoners not to lose weight during his captivity. He was soon thereafter released in a prisoner exchange, was promoted to captain, and went on to fight in the battles at Chancellorsville and Gettysburg among others.

A few months after Gettysburg, in September 1863, Captain Van Buskirk developed a debilitating "Inflammatory Rheumatism" involving his joints and heart, leaving him bedridden. In retrospect, rheumatic fever seems a likely diagnosis, following some streptococcal infection that he might have encountered along the way. He survived but was unable to return to battle and was mustered out the following year.

Despite his lingering illness and disability, David[6d] was able to return to farming with the help of his family. His wife, Lucy, died in 1866. David[6d] married Martha Able the following year and then, after her death in 1873, he married her sister, May Able. After the Civil War was over, P. T. Barnum wanted to exhibit the "Giant" David[6d] Van Buskirk for a substantial salary, but Van Buskirk turned him down flat, content to stay on his Gosport farm.[Du]

Quite active in local politics and community affairs, David[6d] served as county treasurer after the war and ran unsuccessfully for State Treasurer a few years later. He took great pride in the little town of Gosport but often complained that the mainline train, The Limited, did not stop at the Gosport Station. He mused that he might want to go someplace. Thus, on one occasion, it transpired that The Limited did stop when David[6d] needed to travel out of town. It came about when the stationmaster telegraphed ahead to the dispatcher of the Indianapolis and Vincennes Railroad: "Stop Limited at Gosport. Large Party Waiting." No one but David[6d] Van Buskirk got aboard; the angry conductor couldn't really dispute that David[6d] was, indeed, a "large party!"[S]

David[6d] never fully recovered his health, suffering severe rheumatic pains and episodic heart failure with dropsy from which he died on August 12, 1886. They had to build an extra large coffin and widen a door in order to get it out of the house. Then, they added an extra pair of horses to pull the heavy hearse up the hill to the Van Buskirk Graveyard.[Da]

Figure 30. Condensed genealogical chart of Captain David[6d] Van Buskirk, "The Tallest Man in the Union Army," who was descended from the fourth son, Major Thomas[2], of our original patriarch, Laurens[1] Andriessen Van Buskirk. David's first wife was his first cousin.

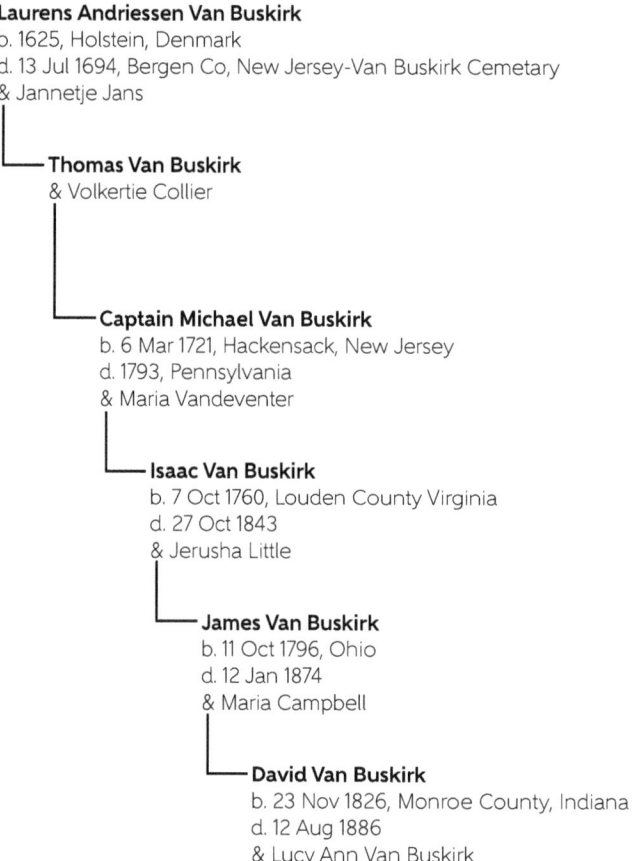

CHAPTER 17

THE BY-WAYS OF DISTANT COUSINS, IV:

The Resurrectionist

PERHAPS THE MOST NOTORIOUS TALE in our family lore of distant cousins concerned the Fort Wayne doctor who dug up graves in the dark of night and was "tarred, feathered, and run out of town on a rail to Deadwood, South Dakota!" Like a lot of lore passed from one generation to the next, the story became a bit exaggerated with repetition, but it sprang from a nidus of fragmented truth. Its roots lay within a conglomerate of fact and fiction that involved at least two different relatives, and was heavily embellished over time. Regardless of the source, it generated intrigue enough to stimulate the curiosity of a young man to pursue the facts for sixty years. It happened like this:

As described with the seventh generation, in 1812, James[7] Van Buskirk immigrated to Ohio as a proverbial babe in his family's arms. His younger brother Jacob[7r] was born thirteen years later in 1825 along the Indian Fork Creek in the Tuscarawas River Valley. In those days, the pioneer farmers frequently had many children: James's parents, Joseph[6] and Rebecca, were no exception with twelve. The younger offspring often were compelled to set out on their own, to pursue a trade, to buy a nearby farm, or to move west. At the same time, the local economy was poor, the summer air, thick with pestilent mosquitoes that carried malaria and yellow fever, and were especially a problem for farmers who tilled the fertile bottomland of the lowland riverbanks. James[7] Van Buskirk moved to northeast Indiana and bought a large and prosperous farm there. James's[7] younger brother, Jacob[7r], had become ill, likely with malaria, endemic among their neighbors in the Tuscarawas Valley.

In the 1850s, the lure of the west was strong, due to its healthier climate, more temperate winters, and available free land, to say nothing of the inherent adventure and even the possibility of finding gold. Most likely for Jacob[7r], it was the hope of improving his health, but regardless of the motivation, in the early 1850s, he and his wife, Mary Ann Elliott, and their four young children, moved west to Indiana. Perhaps they joined his brother James[7] Van Buskirk in northwest Indiana for a time, but Jacob[7r] and his family soon moved on to Aledo, Illinois, just across the Mississippi River from Iowa. I can't help but wonder if they were planning for Aledo to be only a stopping off place before attempting the long trek to the Oregon Territory as did their cousins the William[6ot] Van Buskirks. In the early 1850s, the railroad had been extended west just as far as Aledo on the eastern bank of the Mississippi River. Council Bluffs, Iowa, due west from Aledo across the state of Iowa, was a popular jumping off place across the Missouri River to begin the Oregon Trail. But, they never got further than Aledo. Jacob[7r] became progressively weaker and, in 1857, died of liver failure, likely associated with his primary illness.

Jacob[7r]'s widow, Mary Ann, returned to Ohio with her four young children to be with her family. Her eldest son, Aaron[8r] Elliott Van Buskirk, was eventually "bound out" to an uncle. The term "bound out" generally referred to the practice whereby an impoverished or otherwise incapacitated family would send their child to another family. It was a sort of exchange whereby the youth would work in the new family's farm or trade and would receive food, shelter, and job training. It is, however, possible that he returned to Indiana to live with his father's brother James[7] on the farm, but that is only conjecture. His mother's brother also had a farm near her parents in Ohio and Irene Shoemaker suggests that he first settled in Ohio after returning from Illinois.[S] Regardless, by 1865 Aaron[8r] Elliott Van Buskirk, 18 years of age, had moved back to Monroeville, Indiana, near, if not on, his Uncle James[7] Van Buskirk's farm. Eventually,

Portrait 16. Aaron⁸ʳ Elliott Van Buskirk, MD, professor of surgical anatomy 1847–1904; first cousin to Linford⁸. (Portrait from the family's private collection.)

Aaron's⁸ʳ younger brothers, John Wesley Van Buskirk and Joseph Van Buskirk, as well as their younger sister Mary Belle, all settled in Allen County, Indiana. This accounts for the surfeit of Van Buskirk gravestones both in Fort Wayne and Monroeville in Allen County, Indiana.

In Monroeville, Aaron⁸ʳ Elliott came under the strong influence of his older cousin Joseph⁸ Van Buskirk who was teaching in Monroeville in the 1860s but had great ambitions to become a physician. In the context of the family lore, it was Joseph⁸ Van Buskirk, MD, not Aaron⁸ʳ Elliott, who went to South Dakota, but he went voluntarily, not "tarred and feathered on a rail." Joseph⁸ eventually settled in Rapid City, not Deadwood, to establish his medical practice. To obviate possible confusion, it is well to note that Aaron[8r] Elliott also had a brother named Joseph who became a farmer in Allen County, but it was Aaron's[8r] older cousin Joseph[8] Van Buskirk, MD, who inspired him with the aspirations that he too could become a physician. The lives, education, and medical training of Aaron[8r] Elliott (aka "A.E.") and Joseph[8] Van Buskirk overlapped and intersected for many years with A.E.[8r] always a few steps behind his older cousin, as each struggled to gain an education, earn a medical degree, and maintain a livelihood as a physician. After the Civil War, Joseph[8] Van Buskirk returned to Indiana for a short time, ran a sawmill business and taught in the Monroeville High School where he was succeeded by his younger cousin. A.E.[8r] later joined Joseph[8] in Wisconsin, perhaps to maintain his farm while the elder cousin completed his education. Ultimately, they parted ways. Joseph[8] moved west to the Black Hills of South Dakota where he practiced medicine and ran a drug store.

After a brief teaching stint in central Iowa, A.E.[8r], by 1872, had returned to Ohio to obtain his own medical credentials. A.E.[8r] Van Buskirk taught at the local grammar school in Millersburg, Holmes County, Ohio, where his aunt had come to live after her marriage. In Millersburg, A.E.[8r] Van Buskirk met Mary Jane Gray who was 24 years of age in 1872. She was the daughter of a local scion, Robert Gray, a successful farmer and president of the Holmes County Agricultural Society. The Grays were among Millersburg's most prominent families.

In addition to enjoying the society of Mary Jane Gray, A.E.[8r] was fortunate to meet the most respected physician in Millersburg, Dr. Joel Pomerene, who agreed to take him on as a preceptor. A medical preceptorship was a kind of apprenticeship to a practicing physician who would provide on-the-job training and perhaps lend a book or two from his personal library. Such an arrangement was a common pathway to a medical degree at that time. Dr. Pomerene himself had learned his doctoring at the side of a local Holmes County practitioner, but he eventually graduated in 1858 from Jefferson Medical

College in Philadelphia. He maintained a prominent practice on Main Street in Millersburg; the community hospital now bears his name. Dr. Pomerene became one of the first faculty members in the medical department of Wooster College, about an 18-mile carriage ride north of Millersburg. In 1874, Aaron[8r] Elliott Van Buskirk enrolled in the Wooster Medical Department for one year, probably riding alongside Dr. Pomerene from Millersburg, student and teacher.

After the preceptorship with Dr. Pomerene and the year's course at Wooster, A.E.[8r] qualified for a license to practice medicine. In 1875, he returned to Monroeville, Indiana, where he established his own medical practice. Like many young country doctors struggling to survive, he again taught in the same local high school where his education had begun ten years before. He bought a small house adjacent to the schoolhouse. The small rural town of Monroeville could have supported the farmer-doctor from Ohio, but Aaron[8r] Elliott Van Buskirk, MD, had greater ambitions.

First, the eligible Mary Jane Gray awaited in Millersburg, and A.E.[8r] needed to make clearer plans for a future with her. The apprentice-trained, doctor-farmer, schoolteacher in Indiana may not have had sufficient prospects to encourage the family union. At the same time, some of the physicians in Fort Wayne, the county seat and second largest city in Indiana, had grandiose plans for a regional college of medicine. Although many of the Fort Wayne physicians worried about competition and bickered among themselves, the smaller surrounding rural communities desperately needed knowledgeable doctors. The few physicians who drifted west from the eastern cities were insufficient in number, and often in competence, to fill the need. Over the opposition of a few outspoken colleagues, a circle of Fort Wayne doctors, with the backing of leading citizens, advanced the development of a local medical college. Knowing that Aaron[8r] Elliott Van Buskirk, MD, was part of a local family and had recently obtained his certification in medicine, they approached him about becoming one of the founding faculty. A.E.[8r] jumped at the opportunity, but first wanted to complete his formal training so that he had a full-fledged academic degree in medicine. Thus, he closed the doors of his practice in Monroeville and, in the fall of 1875, Aaron[8r] Elliott Van Buskirk, MD, matriculated in Cincinnati at the Medical College of Ohio, now the College of Medicine of the University of Cincinnati. He graduated in 1876, married Mary Jane Gray, and was immediately recruited to join the faculty as Professor of Surgical Anatomy at the newly inaugurated Fort Wayne College of Medicine.

Unquestionably, serving as a Professor of Anatomy at a medical college offered a fascinating career of teaching and research, as well as prestige among medical colleagues and in the community at large. In the 1870s, in the waning twilight of bloodletting, mercury administration, and purging, anatomy was perhaps the most scientific of all the branches of medicine. It was the core of the medical curriculum. In the minds of prospective students, medical colleges were measured by the quality of the school's anatomy department and especially by the availability of dissection material in the form of human cadavers. The young anatomy professor must also have been aware of the professional risk involved with his new position. The obligation would be his to provide that most crucial commodity for a college of medicine: fresh bodies to be dissected by the medical students. More ominous was the recognition that there really was only one way for the school to obtain those bodies—by means of a shovel on a dark night. No one was exempt, neither pauper nor prince. Thus, just a few months had passed after assuming his position when the young anatomist was called before the school's board of directors to address the vociferous complaints of the medical students. There were insufficient bodies for their dissection. Even the local newspapers reported the unrest at the medical college because the students did not have enough anatomic "subjects" for their dissections.

It happened that not long after his interrogation, A.E.[8r] noted a funeral cortège progressing down the street. Thus, that same night, he managed to arrange with one of the several professional body snatchers, known as "resurrectionists," to meet him outside the Lutheran Cemetery to receive the body of a man that was to be buried that night. Unfortunately, he was seen with several of his students transferring the body into the school's wagon. After some days of investigation, Aaron[8r] Elliott Van Buskirk, MD, was arrested amid community outrage expressed in those same newspapers that had bemoaned the shortage of dissection material just a few weeks before. Of course, the local citizenry were well aware of the likelihood that the bereaved one's body would be stolen. It was a common practice and universal worry in any city near a medical school. All manor of fences, barricades and hired guards were employed to protect the grave (see fig. 31). It usually fell to the graveyard's sextant to protect the grave and to reassure the family that he would keep it safe. However, as often

Figure 31.
Nineteenth-century wrought iron fenced grave in the Roanoke Cemetery, Roanoke, Indiana. Photographed by the author in 2002.

as not, the sexton was in cahoots with the resurrectionists whereby, after the funeral, he would fill the grave with dirt and make some identifying mark in soil, reassuring the family they could check to be sure the mark was there in the morning. Then, later that night, he would help the body snatcher dig up the grave, take out the body, replace the dirt, and replace his mark on the soil.

A.E.[8r] was acquitted of the crime but, during the trial, one of the witnesses had testified that he had seen the same doctor receiving another body a few days before. Immediately after the trial, the police opened the second grave and found it empty. Aaron[8r] Elliott was arrested and tried again for the second body snatch. For that, the newly appointed professor of surgical anatomy was found guilty of what was then the misdemeanor of body snatching and ordered to pay a fine of $50.00. There is no record of his ever having paid the fine. He was neither tarred and feathered nor driven out of town on a rail. He did seem, however, to suffer sufficient professional discomfiture that he and his pregnant wife temporarily retreated back to their small family farm in Millersburg, Ohio.

The difficulty was that, at the time of his trial, there was really no alternative method to obtain cadavers by a school of medicine whether it was Harvard, Columbia, or the Fort Wayne College of Medicine. Ironically, a short while later the paradox was resolved by political pressure induced by a national scandal over the unearthing of the deceased son of a president. The United States Congressman John Scott Harrison, son of the ninth president, William Henry Harrison, and father of the 23rd president, Benjamin Harrison, had died in Cincinnati. When Benjamin Harrison attended the funeral, he and his brother John were asked to help examine the grave of a relative Augustus Devin, who, coincidentally, had been buried nearby on the day before. The soil had been disturbed and they found that the coffin had been opened, the corpse removed. Harrison demanded to inspect the local medical college where he discovered, not the Devin's body, but that of his own father, hanging naked in a laundry chute, waiting to be dissected. The national outcry over the atrocity quickly led to nationwide legislation that mandated the transfer of cadavers

Figure 32. Graves of Dr. Aaron[8r] Elliott Van Buskirk's family with the four small stones of their young children who died in the early 1880s. At left, Aaron[8r] Elliott Van Buskirk, 1847–1904; center, Mary Jane Van Buskirk, 1849–1919; at right, Bess Van Buskirk, 1890–1990. Photographed by the author.

from unclaimed bodies to certified colleges of medicine for anatomic dissection, a practice that continued until late into the twentieth century.

By 1880, Aaron[8r] Elliott and his family returned to Fort Wayne where he regained his position as professor of surgical anatomy. He taught at Fort Wayne Medical College and practiced medicine in Fort Wayne until his untimely death in 1904. The old files tell of the terrible 1880s scarlet fever epidemic in Fort Wayne where A.E.[8r] ministered to the sick children of strangers while his own were dying at home. The pathos of the four miniature gravestones in a line at the feet of their parents' graves persists in my memory (see fig. 32). As evident from the stories told within my family, Aaron[8r] Elliott and his family seemed to carry the stigma of his trial to the end and beyond. Aaron[8r] Elliott Van Buskirk, MD, was eulogized by his colleagues as a prominent Fort Wayne physician who had had a "hard life." His obituary makes no mention of his early disgrace, but the shadow tormented his daughter, Bessie Van Buskirk, throughout her long life. My aunt Alice recollected stories from her childhood about a sad but foreboding old doctor, walking the streets of Fort Wayne in a black cloak and wide brimmed hat. His only surviving daughter, Bessie, in her old age, her own family all deceased, sometimes wrote about the issue to my father, whom she called "uncle." Bessie claimed to her deathbed that they had rung church bells proclaiming her father's innocence, even as she protested, "How were the students to learn?" Perhaps in some form of familial penance, at the age of 100, she committed her own body to be dissected by medical students at Indiana University School of Medicine in 1990.

On the following page:
Figure 33. Genealogical chart showing common ancestry in Joseph[6] Van Buskirk of James[7] and his brother Jacob[7r], father of Aaron[8r] Elliott.

The By-Ways of Distant Cousins, IV: The Resurrectionist

Joseph Van Buskirk
b. 20 Apr 1782, Hamilton Twp, Monroe Co, Pennsylvania
d. 30 May 1864, Warwick Twp, Tuscarawas Co, Ohio
& Rebecca Villars

— **James Van Buskirk**
b. 4 Sep 1811, Pennsylvania
d. 15 Feb 1869
& Annie Morrow

—— **Linford Van Buskirk**
b. 4 Jul 1847, Carroll Co, Ohio
d. 15 Oct 1910, Monroeville, Indiana
& Mary Knouse

——— **Edmund Michael Van Buskirk, MD**
b. 11 Feb 1875, Monroeville, Indiana
d. 18 Jan 1950, Fort Wayne, Indiana
& Mary Louise Schwarze

———— **Edmund Linford Van Buskirk, MD**
b. 15 Oct 1907, Fort Wayne, Indiana
d. 29 Apr 1995, Lafayette, Indiana
& Dorothy Elizabeth Deming

————— **Edmund Michæl Van Buskirk, MD**
b. 13 Jul 1941, Lafayette, Indiana
& Bette Jo Lueck

—— **Joseph Van Buskirk, MD**
b. 8 Feb 1844
d. 10 Nov 1915, Los Angeles, California

— **Jacob Van Buskirk**
b. 1825, Carroll County, Ohio
d. 1857, Mercer County, Illinois
& Mary Ann Elliott

—— **Aaron Elliott Van Buskirk, MD**
b. 27 Sep 1847
d. 21 Jan 1904
& Mary Jane Gray

—— **John Wesley Van Buskirk**
b. 15 Apr 1853, Monroeville, Indiana
d. 11 Jan 1913, Monroeville, Indiana
& Matilda Emily Edwards

—— **Joseph Van Buskirk**
& Elmira Riley

—— **Mary Belle Van Buskirk**
b. 1857
& Samuel Isenberger

CHAPTER 18

THE ELEVENTH GENERATION:

Edmund Michael Van Buskirk (1941-   )

I HAVE ARRIVED at that odd point in the narrative whereby I find myself describing that individual that I should know best, but consider: "If only we could see ourselves . . . !" Despite an imperfect self-perception, I can describe with relative accuracy those experiences that molded and influenced my life so far. I have attempted to include in this narrative as much information as I could verify and that was pertinent to our ancestors in each generation. For that, my task was made relatively easy by my father and grandfather who, long before anyone had even dreamed of the internet and genealogical websites, had traced the entirety of our direct male genealogical line back to its New World progenitor, Laurens[1] Andriessen Van Buskirk.

I recall from around 1970 receiving a bulky manila document packet from my father that contained some old facsimile genealogical charts as well as a completely filled out application for my membership in the Holland Society of New York. The accompanying letter from my father explained that the Holland Society was for male direct descendants of the original Dutch colony of New Netherlands with instructions of where I should sign before mailing. They had done the hard part by determining our direct genealogical line to New Netherlands. All I needed was to verify some of the early references and to include as much newly acquired information as the many recent resources have made possible. At first, it was cold historical facts: records of births,

The Eleventh Generation: Edmund Michael Van Buskirk (1941-)

marriages, property, and deaths. By the Revolutionary War, it became even more personal to discover that no less than six members of one family had fought in that struggle (George[4] and his five sons) and to read their names on the individual muster lists of the Northampton Militia Battalions, now held in the Pennsylvania State Archives. By the same token, one experiences some mild genealogical discomfiture to learn about the many Loyalists who chose to side with the British, fighting their relatives over the fate of their ancestors' adopted land in the midst of their own and their neighbors' frenetic choice whether to fight or not. The toll of progress becomes even more compelling when reading, in Andrew[7ot] Van Buskirk's own hand, of the Van Buskirk horrific struggles across the plains and mountains of the Oregon Trail, burying his own mother in a shallow grave among the shale-laden ruts of those who had gone before. I found myself drawn to the grave of this Andrew[7ot] and his family in Amity, Oregon, much as I was compelled to finish the engraving on the Indiana gravestone of A.E.[8r] Van Buskirk's daughter, Bessie, the last of her family's direct line.

By the genealogical time of the Civil War, for the first time, I read of people about whom I had heard direct conversations and seen in family pictures since I was a child: George[8], killed at Gettysburg before his twenty-first birthday; Joseph[8], who became a physician in South Dakota; even the giant distant cousin from Gosport, David[6d], "tallest man in the Union Army." With the next generation, my narrative begins to concern people that I remember seeing and hearing, with vague memories of visiting their homes. And, finally one arrives at parents, siblings, and self where objectivity loosens its grip, where verifiable facts, dates, and places inexorably intertwine with lore, anecdote, and emotion.

Edmund[11] Michael Van Buskirk was born to Edmund[10] Linford and Dorothy Elizabeth Deming Van Buskirk on July 13, 1941. My dad always said that I "walked in the front door" because I weighed 10.5 pounds at birth. By that time, my parents and my two older sisters, Nancy[11] Louise and Joan[11] Elizabeth had moved to Lafayette, Indiana, where my father had established his ophthalmological and otolaryngological practice at the Arnett-Crockett Clinic. They had just completed a new home in an area of West Lafayette called "Hills and Dales," near the campus of Purdue University.

In December of 1941, the Japanese bombed Pearl Harbor, and the United States officially entered World War II. But something else occupied my parents' attention: their 5-month-old baby lay mortally ill in the hospital with an acute abdomen. Fortunately, my godfather and founder of the Arnett Clinic, Dr. A.C. Arnett, astutely diagnosed a Meckel's diverticulum, an uncommon congenital pouch-like anomaly of the large intestine that had undergone intussusception, a telescoping into the adjacent cavity of the large bowel. His diagnostic acumen and emergency surgery saved my infant life. When my dad asked A.C. if he should remove my appendix, the wise old surgeon simply said, "The kid's had enough." It proved to be the first of the fortuitous encounters with extraordinary people who have graced my existence since that fateful time.

From early childhood, I had a heavy dose of the medical field: I was literally surrounded by physicians—my father, my grandfather, and my father's clinic colleagues. I seemed destined to become the fourth generation of physicians, the fifth when you include that pioneer root doctor back in eastern Ohio, Anne Elizabeth (Cree) Van Buskirk. I remember so well from early childhood making hospital bedside rounds with my father, Dr. Van, as the sisters and nurses called him. At the old Catholic hospital, he would enter through the rear of the building, greet the Sister Superior, and hang his coat in her office. Looming from the folds of her mysterious habit, Sister would always smile down upon me. Sometimes she would wait with me in the hospital corridor while my father made his rounds from room to room. On occasion, he would bring me to the patient's bedside where I would watch in awe or horror, as he would change dressings and otherwise minister to invariably grateful people. I still recall my mother admonishing me as a very little boy to be polite or, "What will your patients think?" I have no doubt that I learned what came to be called "bedside manner" at a very early age. In my lifetime, I was rather sad to see

The Eleventh Generation: Edmund Michael Van Buskirk (1941-)

Portrait 17. Edmund[11] Michael Van Buskirk, age 3, with father, 1944.

Portraits 17–21 and Figs. 35–37 from the author's private collection.

hospital rounds of the ophthalmologist go the way of calomel and bloodletting when most eye surgery moved out of the hospital to become an outpatient procedure done in isolation from other medical colleagues. Regardless of the setting, I never forgot the bedside lessons of my father's example.

Portrait 18. Van Buskirk Family, 1949. This photograph was taken on the property of an old farm restaurant in Williamsport, Indiana, known in our family as "Mother Has" because the owner's daughters always announced the day's menu with "Mother has!" Edmund[11] Michael Van Buskirk is the 8-year-old boy in front, then, left to right: older sister, Nancy[11] Louise; mother, Dorothy Elizabeth; sister, Joan[11] Elizabeth; father, Edmund[10] Linford, 1949.

I attended a small public high school down the street from my house. Most of the students were kids of Purdue University professors who demanded at least a modicum of academic rigor. It was then that I first became involved in medical research.

Like most 15-year-olds, my mind was also on sports, and I thought I had found an affinity for track and field: soon, however, I soon injured my foot. Once again, a medical experience brought an encounter with another extraordinary mentor. An elderly family doctor, "Doc Holiday" no less, tended my injury with his prescient 1950s' interest in "sports medicine." He recommended that I meet the local FBI agent, Fred Wilt, who had been an Olympic runner in 1948 London games and in 1952 in Helsinki. Fred still trained a few young athletes. After long talks, long runs, and careful scrutiny on his part (I think to be sure this doctor's son wasn't too soft), he agreed to take me on.

I began a three-year tutorial with Fred in what was supposed to be training for track but really became preparation for life. Because I had been raised in quite comfortable circumstances in a sanguine era, I had never really struggled at the outer fringe of exertion and desire before. Fred's initial reservations were undoubtedly well founded. At the time, I did not realize that he was revered in the world of track and field. He had won the Sullivan Award for best American amateur athlete in 1950, and was a member of the Track and Field Hall of Fame. He had become a successful FBI agent and was locally renowned for having cleaned up organized crime in Lafayette. He would use metaphors from that side of his work to inspire me. Even criminals, he explained, to be successful in what they do, "have to live in the gutter and throw their Kewpie doll in the gutter!" Thus, he expounded, no matter what path you follow, you must immerse yourself in the endeavor to the limits of your tolerance and endurance. I trained everyday for three years, rain or shine, hot or cold, running on weekends over empty golf courses or obscure country roads, long before running became fashionable. Most winter weekdays Fred met me at the Purdue indoor track at 6:00 p.m. I never knew what arrangements he made, either with Purdue or with my father, for us to be there. I do know that Fred always greeted me with "Hello, Athlete!"

Fred experimented with a variety of training techniques, including early trials of interval training. He gave me a new schedule each week, accelerating the pace of the intervals each time. I recall running twenty quarter-miles at a sixty-second pace, jogging a lap between. I don't think I ever really mastered his methods, but I certainly became extraordinarily fit. On one occasion, he was pushing me extra hard, and I couldn't understand why, in spite of all the training, I was so exhausted. His blue eyes penetrated mine while his words seared my sensorium with the maxim: "Training doesn't make it easy; it just makes it possible." Those few words sustained me through many a grueling run, but more so later on, through long nights of preparing for a medical and research career. Fred constantly stressed preparation of the mind as well as the body, telling me that it took three months to prepare the body to run a four-minute mile, but another nine to prepare the mind. He would also tell me when you were near the finish line, it didn't matter how you felt because "the heat of passion will bring you in!" And though I went off to college and pursued a different path, memories of his maxims always inspired, sustained, and bolstered me. I hope he knew how much he had influenced my life.

In 1959, I matriculated at Harvard College in Cambridge, Mass., and never again returned to Indiana for more than a week or so. Of course, the new horizons that were visible and palpable in Cambridge temporarily diverted medicine to the bottom of my list for subjects I wanted to study. Harvard didn't offer a "pre-medical" program because college was for education of the young, not to provide vocational training. I was able to take biology classes under two Nobel Laureates—George Wald and James Watson. But I became more entranced by anthropology than by pure biology. I studied and received a bachelor of arts (1963) and a master's degree (1964) under Professor William White Howells, whose research, among other things, had demonstrated definitively that all human beings are of the same species, a topic anachronistically still controversial at the time. I used to wonder why we spent so much time on taxonomy because I did not realize the extent of my mentor's own interests and contributions. For me, it was another fortunate encounter with a scholar and gentleman who was always graceful and kind to me, even when I decided I wanted to go to medical school after all.

The Eleventh Generation: Edmund Michael Van Buskirk (1941-)

Portrait 19.
Edmund[11] Michael Van Buskirk, Harvard College Graduation, 1963.

In the spring of 1964, the most important chance encounter of my life came one Saturday afternoon by way of a telephone call from my old college roommate inquiring about my evening plans. It seemed that a former classmate was in town, and I was needed as a date for his sister. Lucky again for me, the classmate spent the evening talking to his sister, while I became smitten with his date, one Bette Jo Lueck of Flint, Michigan. Three days later, Bette accompanied me to a Harvard hockey game, and three months later we were engaged to be married. She was in graduate school in special education and ultimately received master's degrees in education of the deaf and the deaf-blind, both from Boston University and from Smith College. Unbeknown to her, I taught myself sign language from the dictionary. When she started to sign again on our next date, I said, "I can read that!" She handed me one of those little cards with the alphabetical signs. I glanced at it and told her, "I've got them!" She tested me with a brief sentence, and I rattled off the translation. It worked! We were married on June 19, 1965, and were looking forward to the long and happy life we have shared together, now for 53 years.

In the fall of 1964, I matriculated at Boston University School of Medicine where another medical encounter proved to be life changing. I had already had quite a bit of exposure to ophthalmology, and I wanted to explore other fields. However, when I stayed up studying late one night, my contact lenses abraded the surface of my eye. By chance, the nation's youngest ophthalmology department chairman, Ephraim Friedman, saw me and fixed up not just my scratched eye, but, more important, my life's work. I had found myself another mentor, and soon I was working in his lab, learning the latest discoveries in the field of ophthalmology. Eph influenced most of the important professional decisions I made throughout my career. He was instrumental in directing me

Figure 34. Graduation from Boston University School of Medicine, 1968, with two of my more important mentors: my father, Edmund[10] L. Van Buskirk, MD, at right; and Dean Ephraim Friedman, MD, in the middle.

to a career in research, and he always encouraged his students to take a purely academic approach to medical issues. My fellow classmates and I quickly learned never to ask a question the answer to which we easily could find in the library first, after which he was happy to discuss, question, and elaborate. When asked about a clinical case, he would invariably turn to his blackboard and draw tissue cross-sections of the pathological cause, as if we were looking at a pathology slide under a microscope. Eph often reminded me that one can always receive more clinical training, but it is difficult to return from the clinic to research laboratory. Now, forty odd years later, when I encounter list-checking, incurious, and robotic doctors, I can only think of how they could have benefited from Ephraim Friedman's tutelage.

I went on to study and practice in the ophthalmic subspecialty of glaucoma, spending my professional days with challenging clinical problems, conducting research, writing research articles, and traveling the world speaking and learning about glaucoma.

In the course of nearly forty years of ophthalmology, I wrote or edited seven books, published over 200 scientific articles, editorials, and book chapters, and was the founding editor of the *Journal of Glaucoma*. I served as president of the American Glaucoma Society. Over the years, I managed to accumulate a few honors, beginning with the Dumphy Eye Research Fellowship at Massachusetts Eye and Ear Infirmary in 1973 and, perhaps most crucial to my ultimate career, a Research Career Development Award that provided me with five years of support from the National Institutes of Health in 1976. Among the various honorary lectures I was privileged to present, most memorable were the Chandler-Grant Lecture at Mass. Eye and Ear Infirmary in 1994, the Robert N. Shaffer Lecture at the Annual Meeting of the American Academy of Ophthalmology in 1996, receipt of the Fankhouser Medal from the University of Basel in 2003, and a Distinguished Alumni Award from the Department of Ophthalmology, Harvard University Medical School in 2007.

Figure 35. On the Occasion of being Guest of Honor at the Annual Meeting of the American Glaucoma Society, 2006. Edmund[11] Michael Van Buskirk, MD with family: left to right: wife, mother, and Nana, Bette Jo; grandson Luke Edmund; Edmund Michael; daughters Sarah Lynn, Amy Louise, and Audrey Elisabeth.

Despite these various accolades, looking back from the perspective of my ophthalmic retirement, my own tangible body of work pales in my heart compared to the accomplishments of my students whom I might have influenced. These astute clinicians, contributors to the collective body of scientific knowledge, chairs of academic departments, and a university president surely owe some of their own successes to the influence of Edmund[10] L. Van Buskirk, Fred Wilt, William Howells, Ephraim Friedman, and so many others who inspired me. Perhaps a half-dozen such mentors immeasurably enriched my life, guiding me to fresh endeavors that I otherwise may not have undertaken. It had begun with my father from whom I learned much about life, history, and medicine, and who always reinforced the idea in me that "life is a continuous process of education." Primarily a practicing physician in a small Hoosier town, he continuously inspired me to expand my professional and intellectual horizons, not just in a quest for knowledge, but also for the inviolate obligation to share that knowledge with anyone who needed it. I would never have been able to accomplish what I did in my life without him and my other mentors who unselfishly shared with me their skills, time, and knowledge. I long understood that the only available avenue for repayment was to do the same for those students who came under my influence and tutelage. Those of us who have reaped such benefit at the side of great teachers must surely carry with us a sacrosanct obligation to extend their trust to our own students and colleagues. By the time of my retirement, I found abhorrent the vanity and avarice manifest in some members of my profession, but my deepest disdain remains for those who withhold their knowledge and technical skill from their colleagues, or sell it in bits at exorbitant rates in order to maintain a competitive advantage.

As I approached my seventh decade, I began once again to look beyond my established situation and to explore long dormant instincts. The gift of an old Argus "A" 35mm camera in the 1940s became the nidus for a lifelong passion for photography, not just taking pictures but especially to create the ingredients for making photographic prints in my own darkroom laboratory. Fifty years later, the expansive new possibilities of the digital age rekindled that passion in the forefront of my mind, and I began to study digital imagery in some detail. In 2004, it seemed to be the logical time for me to move on. I closed the door on ophthalmology to pursue my rekindled passion for photographic printing. Arthur Conan Doyle, through his protagonist in *The Greek Interpreter* exclaims: "Art in the blood is liable to take the strangest forms."[Doy]

Some of it must have seeped down to me. My grandfather and namesake was a skilled pen and ink artist. My father had the skill if not the time or inclination. My sister Joan Van Buskirk Tanner, is a widely known and respected California artist whose new and older work continues to be exhibited throughout the country. Thus, it was not surprising to me when I felt drawn in that direction and was enchanted to be free to pursue it.

Bette and I have three daughters: Audrey Elizabeth, born January 15, 1968; Sarah Lynn, born January 1, 1972, and Amy Louise, born January 5, 1974. They were all born in what was then called the Boston Lying-In Hospital; all are now married and have brought us ten grandchildren, nine boys and one girl. Their stories of the twelfth generation and beyond will come from their own able hands and will arise from within when they reach that contemplative age for telling their own tales.

Portrait 20. Edmund[11] Michael Van Buskirk, MD (1941–). Photographed at Duke University School of Medicine, 2003.

Portrait 21. Edmund[11] Michael Van Buskirk, MD (1941–). Photographed at age 73, in 2014.

Figure 36. Photographed in 2015 at Brasada Ranch, Oregon, on the 50th Wedding Anniversary of Bette and Edmund[11] Michael Van Buskirk. Back row, left to right: Amy Van Buskirk Théry, François Théry, Bette Van Buskirk, Violet Gullung, Audrey Van Buskirk Lydgate, Chris Lydgate, Sarah Van Buskirk Gullung, Walter Gullung, Charles Gullung. Front row, left to right: Noah Gullung, Luke Van Buskirk, Hank Gullung, Alex Lydgate, Theo Lydgate, Benjamin Théry, Nicolas Théry, Charlie Gullung, and Michael Van Buskirk.

Figure 37. Descendants of Bette Jo Lueck and Edmund[11] Michael Van Buskirk.

Edmund Michæl Van Buskirk, MD
b. 13 Jul 1941, Lafayette, Indiana
& Bette Jo Lueck, b. 9 Aug 1941

- **Audrey Elizabeth Van Buskirk**
  b. 15 Jan 1968, Boston, Massachusetts
  & Hugh Forrest
  - **Luke Edmund Van Buskirk**
    b. 9 Dec 1999, Emanuel Hospital, Portland, Oregon
- **Audrey Elizabeth Van Buskirk**
  b. 15 Jan 1968, Boston, Massachusetts
  & Christopher John Lydgate
  - **Theodore Edmund Lydgate**
    b. 10 Jun 2007, Portland, Oregon
  - **Alexander Edmund Lydgate**
    b. 18 Jan 2009, Portland, Oregon
- **Sarah Lynn Van Buskirk**
  b. 1 Jan 1972, Boston, Massachusetts
  & Charles William Gullung
  - **Violet Henrietta Gullung**
    b. 2 Jul 2003, New York, New York
  - **Charles Michæl Gullung**
    b. 11 Feb 2005, Emanual Hospital, Portland, Oregon
  - **John Henry Gullung**
    b. 3 Apr 2007, Emanual Hospital, Portland, Oregon
  - **Noah Wliiiam Gullung**
    b. 23 May 2009, Emanual Hospital, Portland, Oregon
  - **Walter Edward Lueck Gullung**
    b. 8 Oct 2011, Emanual Hospital, Portland, Oregon
- **Amy Louise Van Buskirk**
  b. 5 Jan 1974, Boston, Massachusetts
  & Francois Étienne Thery
  - **Benjamin Franck Emile Thery**
    b. 29 Jan 2008, New York, New York
  - **Nicolas Edmund Thery**
    b. 21 Aug 2009, UCSF Hospital, San Francisco, California

BIBLIOGRAPHY

AL. Arrowsmith & Lewis's *New and Elegant General Atlas*, 1st ed. Philadelphia, John Conrad & Co.; editions were published in 1804, 1805, 1812, and 1819 per Lister. Although published in 1804, the map is dated 1800–1803 by counties shown, and the same identical map was published in all later editions of the atlas. Retrieved from http://www.mapsofpa.com/.

Ba. Barry, Louise. *The Beginning of the West. Annals of the Kansas Gateway to the American West 1540–1854*, 1st ed. Kansas State Historical Society, 1972.

B. Braisted, Todd W. "How George Washington Saved the Life of Abraham Van Buskirk's Son." *Journal of the American Revolution* (Sept. 2014). Online at https://allthingsliberty.com/2014/09/how-george-washington-saved-the-life-of-abraham-van-buskirks-son/.

D. Davis, W. W. H. *The History of Bucks County, Pennsylvania*. Doylestown, Pa.: Democrat Book and Job Office Print, 1876. Online at https://books.google.com/books/about/The_History_of_Bucks_County_Pennsylvania.html?id=bwtNS1C8ljwC.

Da. Datzman, Richard C. "The Tallest Union Soldier in the Civil War," *Indiana History Bulletin*, Vol. 51, No. 3 (March 1974).

Do. Dollarhide, William, *Map Guide to American Migration Routes, 1735–1815*. Bountiful, Utah: Heritage Quest, 2000.

Doy. Doyle, Sir Arthur Conan and Baring-Gould, William S., editor, *The Greek Interpreter, The Annotated Sherlock Holmes: The Four Novels and Fifty-Six Short Stories*. New York: Clarkson N. Potter, 1978.

Du. Durham, Roger S. "The Biggest Yankee in the World," *The Civil War Times, Illustrated* (May 1974): pp. 28–33.

F. Firestone, William. *Grandeur and Grace in the Ohio Country, Building America from the Ground Up, 1784–1860*. Yellow Springs, Ohio: Red Eft Media, 2009. Accessed from blog post at Red Eft Media Blog Spot, http://s355168980.onlinehome.us/2011/05/28/grandeur-and-grace-in-the-ohio-country-building-america-from-the-ground-up-1784-1860/.

Fl. Flint, Rosalie Viola Matthews and Tesh, Alice May Matthews. *Our Matthews, Van Buskirk and Whisler Ancestors*. Limited edition. Wenatchee, Washington: R.V. M. Flint, 1981.

Ga. Gaston, Joseph. *The Centennial History of Oregon, 1811–1912*. Chicago: S.J. Publishing Co., 1912. Accessed online at ancestry.com.

H. Hardesty, H. H. *Illustrated Historical Atlas—Carroll County, Ohio*. Chicago: H.H. Hardesty, 1874.

Hi. Historic American Buildings Survey, Creator. *Thomas Van Buskirk House, East Saddle River Road, Saddle River, Bergen County, NJ*. Bergen County New Jersey Saddle River, 1933. Documentation Compiled After. Photograph. https://www.loc.gov/item/nj0274/.

Ho. Hopkins, G. M. & G.M. Hopkins & Co. (1873), combined atlas of the state of New Jersey and the late township of Greenville, now part of Jersey City, from actual survey official records and private plans. Philadelphia: G.M. Hopkins & Co. [Map] Retrieved from the Library of Congress, https://www.loc.gov/item/2007626870/.

Hu. Hurt, R. Douglas. *The Ohio Frontier. Crucible of the Old Northwest, 1720–1830*. Bloomington and Indianapolis, Indiana: Univ. Press, 1998.

J. Jones, Wilbur D. *Giants of the Cornfields the 27th Indiana Infantry*. Shippensburg, Pa.: White Mane Publishing Co., 1997.

K. King, Wilbur Lewis. *Knauss Genealogy: Lukas Knauss (1633–1713) of Dudelsheim, Germany, and his American Descendants*. Bethlehem, Pa.: privately printed, 1930.

L. Lackey, Howard L. *The Tenmile Country and Its Pioneer Families*. 3rd printing. Apollo, Pa.: Closson Press, 2001.

M. Mann, Charles C. *1491: New Revelations of the Americas before Columbus*. New York: Alfred A. Knopf, 2005.

Ma. Mattes, Merrill J. *Platte River Road Narratives*. Chicago: Univ. Ill. Press, 1988.

Mi. Miller, Charles H. *Historic Families of America*. Chicago: Charles Kingsbury Miller, 1897.

Mo. Morris, Harvery. "Washington County Giants." *Indiana Historical Society Publications*, Vol 7, no 8, 1921.

N. Nelson, William. "The Founder of the Van Buskirk Family in America." *Proceedings of the New Jersey Historical Society*. In Four Parts: Vol III, No 6, July 1906; Vol IV, No 1, Oct 1906; Vol IV No 2, Jan–April 1907; Vol V, No 3, Jul–Oct 1908.

Pe. Pennsylvania Evening Post, Oct.1, 1776.

S. Shoemaker, Irene English. *Van Buskirk; a Legacy from New Amsterdam*. Anderson, Indiana: Business Printing, 1990.

Sa. Sabine, Lorenzo. *Biographical Sketches of Loyalists of the American Revolution with an Historical Essay*. Boston: Little Brown & Co, 1864.

Sc. Schilling, Robert Wilson. *The Yellow Creek Stories*. Toronto, Ohio: Robert Wilson Schilling, 1947.

Bibliography

Sh. Shorto, Russell. *The Island at the Center of the World*. New York: Doubleday, 2004.

Sp. Shepherd, William R. *Historical Atlas*. New York: Henry Holt and Company, 1911.

T. Thomas, Joseph. "A Synopsis of the History of Moreland Township and Grove. Upper Moreland Historical Association." PDF at http://www.umha.com/PDFs/ Synopis_of UM.pdf.

Ta. *The Times Atlas of the World, Eighth Comprehensive Edition, New York and Environs*. New York: Random House, 1990, Plate 103.

Tr. Trinklein, Michael J. *The Oregon Trail*. Amazon Digital Services, Michael J. Trinklein, 2011.

V. Van der Donck, Adriaen. *A Description of The New Netherlands*, edited by Thomas F. O'Donnell. Syracuse, N.Y.: Syracuse University Press, 1968.

W. Winfield, Charles H. *History of the County of Hudson, New Jersey*. New York: Kennard and Hay Stationery M'fg and Printing Co, 1874.

W2. Winfield, Charles H. *History of the Land Titles of Hudson County, N.J. 1609–1871*. New York: Whykoop & Hallenback Printers, 1872.

Wa. Wallace, Paul A. W. *Indian Paths of Pennsylvania*. 2nd printing. The Pennsylvania Historical and Museum Commission, 1971.

Wh. Whitcomb, Royden Page. *First History of Bayonne, New Jersey*. Bayonne, N.J.: R.P. Whitcomb, 1904.

Wns. "A Brief History of New Sweden in America." The Swedish Colonial Society. Online at www.colonialswedes.net/History/History.htm.

APPENDIX

ANDREW VAN BUSKIRK'S JOURNAL

The following is an exact transcript from *The William Van Buskirk Family Trek on the Oregon Trail*, which covers the period of October 1851–October 1852. It is shown with the original spelling and punctuation and is reproduced with permission from Juliette Hyatt, from her Ancestry.com posting. Spaces between entry dates have been added for ease of reading.

Oct 2d 1851

William and Margaretta Vanbuskirk with their entire family of 6 children, 2 sons in law, 2 daughters in law, 11 grandchildren left their good homes in Knox and Morrow County, Ohio with the intention of crossing the plains to the great Oregon. Six of our dear ones died and was buried as best we could how sad, yes sad is not enough it allmost took our lives to leave our dear ones in such a way but we shal meet them over on the other bright shore where our hearts will not be sad there will be no plains to cross! no sad burials to endure but our loved ones will be there

Knox County Ohio to Franklin to Pulaskiville

Oct 2nd 1851

started from home passed through Pulaskiville, and Chesterville, nothing happened

3: Passed through east Liberty and Olivegreen & staid all knight at Sunberry Delaware County

4: Left Sunberry and had a little scrape about the dog, and then passed Galena and Westerville and drove with 1/2 mile of Columbus and staid all knight.

Passed Columbus, crossed the Scioto, passed Rome and Holton, then to Jefferson in Madison County ... Passed Lafayette & Sumerford, Brighton, Viena, and Springfield of Clark County ... Passed Midway, crossed Mad river ... Passed New Lebanon, and Jonesville in montgomery Co, passed Westville of Prebel County and then passed the state line ... Indiana. staid all knight at cousin Wm Vanburkirks. Passed .... Greenville of Hancock Co ... passed Indianopolis, and crossed white river ... passed Bellevill ... Pulmansville of Putnam Co. and stayed all night and the gray mare got hurt in the wagoon wheel ... passed Manhattan ... worst roads that we traveled ... passed through Terrehaute and crossed the Wabash ... Passed Pari Edgar County in Illinois ... Passed through a large prairai ... passed several small Praireis in Christian County ... Crossed Sangamon river ... Berlin ... crossed the Illinois river at Phillips Ferry ... stayed all knight within 14 miles of the Mississippi river.

Oct 26:

Went to the Mississippi river and camped on the bank at knight ... Crossed the Mississippi river at Hanibal ferried 7 miles and ... went through a little town with no boddy living in it ... Passed through Shelbyville 15 miles & staid all knight and got the gray mare kicked bad. Drove 5 miles and put up and doctored the mare and bought a horse....

Nov 3:

Swapped horses and then passed through Chilicothe.... Went through Gallatin forded the west fork of Grand river Crossed the Sandstone creek... Passed Rochester... & landed at the Vanbuskirk settlement

Nothing happened through the winter worth mentioning.

April 29th 1852

Crossed the Missouri river at Elizabethtown, and started for Oregon, an traveled on about a hundred miles. and the company was in perfect confusion and quarreling, on the knight of May 13th we staid on Wolf Creek, and I found a bee tree, and saw a great many Indians. traveled 15 miles and camped. an Indian had been shot the day before and we expected danger... Traveled 15 miless... the road was crouded with waggons. Traveled 5 and E.F. Whislers teem took a stampeed, but no particular damage done. Traveled 10 and our teems all took a stampeed except Josephs and Fathers, Whislers teem wasbehind and mine next, and Whislers teem scared mine and then it run but noboddy seriously hurt, our teems stampeeded twice on the same day. Remained in camp, and washed repaired one yokes and picketed our cattle.... Traveled up the Blue about 15 miles and camped, saw where a man had been shot.... Drove 15 miles and camped in the bluffs of Platte river... The Platte is a beautiful River it looks something like the Mississippi, but not much depth of water but little timber on the south side. . . . I have been unwell for 2 or 3 days. now on the mend. Drove 18 miles and camped found wood plenty but green . . . I still remain unwell with dysentary.

May 28:

Drove 20 miles, Whisler, Snyder, and myself went out on a hunting expedition. we saw game plenty but I was so sick that when I would get off of my horse to shoot I could not hold the gun to my face, that spoiled hunting for some time. . . . Traveled 20 miles crossed the bluffs without water or grass. . . . had a very hard days drive . . . descended the bluffs of Platte the rode was all sand . . . all sand. . . drove 18 miles principlly all sand. Drove 18 miles through a considerable sand, and Snyder was taken with colery [cholera], or a similar disease. Remained in camp on account of Snyder being sick. Drove 16 miles Sarah Whisler sick. Drove 18 miles and camped opposite the chimney rok it is said to be 600 feet high it makes a very beautiful appearance. Drove 12 miles, stopped at noon Snyder died we buried him Tenmiles west of the chimney rock. . . . passed through Scotts bluff it - - - they were a very romantic sight. . . . John was sick with dysentery . . . remained in camp, Wm. V. Whisler being sick. . . . camped without any grass. Drove 8 miles in the black hills and camped . . . camped on the Labonde River --- a beautiful stream it was. . . . red hills the ground in the road was as red as ever paint was.

June 26:

. . . passed Independence rock and the Devils gate & crossed the Sweet water independence rock is just single rock, a small

Mountain, standing deperate and apart from any other rock or mountain. it's situated between the road and the river. . . . camped on strawberry creek crossed the sweet water 4 times. Drove 16 miles crossed the Sweet water again found plenty of snow. Remained in camp to recruit our catte, we had ice in the buckets last knight. Took the South . . . of summit of the Rockey Mountains . . . camped on little Sandy. . . . our cattles feet are getting well worn.

Remained incamp, drove the cattle 5 miles to grass, poor at that prepaired for crossing the desert on Subletts cutoff. Margaret . . . sick; & Joshua Hardy sick.

July 7:

Drove 28 miles by driving until 10 o'clock at knight. Drove 12 miles ferried Green river and camped on Blacks fork. The cattle had no water from the time crossed Sandy until we got to Green river being 46 miles, 60 hours without water. Remained in camp to recruit our cattle and the boys cut their waggon beds off. . . bought a steer for Father for $30.00. . . . Drove 16 miles over verry steep mountains and camped on muddy fork of Bear river near the mouth. . . . Drove 19 miles, and camped on Falls creek of Bear river, found the grave of R.F. McCracken from Chester Township Ohio and we repaired his grave according to the wishes of his Father and we camped within 40 rods E.F. Whisler and his horses strayed from him --- Drove 5 miles. Staid behind with Whisler to search for his horses, it being that he had gave them up. I was lucky in the pursuit, found the horses and brought them in to camp by the middle of the afternoon I then went to our camp and Whisler bore my company until I saw our waggons a 1/2 mile off to the right of the road . . . . passed the soda and Steamboat springs, and left the California road took the Oregon road to the right.

July 21:

Remained in amp till aftr noon. Arminda verry sick and our cattle all sick and vomiting. I suppose they had got some poisonour herb, or water, hitched up and drove 6 miles and camped . . . cattle yet sick remained in camp all day and drenched our cattle. . . . Passed fort hall drove 17 miles an crossed a branch of Snake river Weeks left the train. . . . drove 9 miles and camped on Raft river and it was one of he dustiest t imes that I most ever saw. . . Hoppin left the train.

Aug 2:

Drove 17 miles, and camped on a little run with water in pools. . . . set my waggon tire. . . . camped on the river again Whisler drove up his cattle in the morning independent of all, and left the company but we camped within 1/4 mile of him on the knight, and John went to his cmap in the evening to know what he meant by leaving in the way he did, and he said that he expected that we would drive on where he did that knight and John said that we did not know what his calculation was but expected he was a going on to leave us and said on the 7th he did intend to go right on we remained in camp on account of Joseph and Mary VanBuskirk being sick, and Whisler drove past while we was eating breakfast near Salmon falls. . . . Remained in camp till noon and J Hardy left us . . . drove . . . to the old crossing of Snake River to go to fort Boise and camped. Remained in camp on account of sickness. . . . J. T. and Mary VanBuskirk, verry sick yet.

Aug 14:

Remained in camp. in the morning about 4 o'clock Joseph T. VanBuskirk departed this life, we buried him on the same day, near camp near the lower crossing of Lewis on Snake River to go to Fort Boise on the south side of the river between the river and the road, on the top of the first hill or raise from the river bottom 1/4 mile from where we ascended the hill and about 200 years from the road, right opposite the grave there is an island in the river, from 1/2 to 1 mile long from where we pastured our stock for several days the slough of hte river near 100 yards wide but no trouble to ford it from the grave to the island 1$ mile or upwards. [I think he went into great details so that someone could find the grave.]

Aug 14:

in 2 miles and a half the road comest o the river again, Mary Vanbuskirk died late in the afternoon, on the morning of the 15th we buried her by the side of her Father.

Aug 16:

Drove 12 miles bad road with rock -- broke my waggon tongue.

Aug 17:

Remained in camp and threw away one waggon ...

Aug 19:

Drove 7 miles by noon. remained in camp in the after noon Sarah P. Vanbuskirk verry sick

Aug 20:

Remained in camp til 4'oclock drove 8 miles Sarah P. Vanbuskirk departed this life we buried her about 42 miles from the other graves on a level plain on the river bottom 1/2 mile from the river, about 100 yards from the road on the left hand of the road going west hill 1/4 mile off to the left, on river bottom; on the other side of the river pependicular bluffs somewhat ragged appearance. with white places perhaps sand, came to the river in 4 miles from where she was buried, it was all clay ground for some distance sand hills on the left. . . . one steer died . . drove without grass or water . . . drove and camped . . . warm spring warm enough for dish water . . . drove and camped Elizabeth Henderson sick. . . drove and passed Boise . . . drove and came to burnt river crossed Birch creek . . . camped on Powder rive slough . . .

Sept 20:

Drove 3 miles and camped without water we are not in the Blue montains most all sick hardly able to take care of each other I have been cook some time

Sept 23:

Drove 4 miles and camped Mother departed this life about 8 o'clock in the evening

Sept 24:

Remained in camp and buried Mother, we dug the grave through a shelly limestone rock, in the Blue mountains 4 miles before we came to Arrow creek, on a small Prairai on opening near the root of a large yellow pine tree and some other trees of the same kind near the road within 50 yards timber near on both sides of the road the timber was principally fir and pine she is buried on the north side of the road . . . .

Sept 26:

Drove . . . camped . . . lost the old mare . . . .

Oct 2:

Drove 6 miles by noon and then remained in camp and in the evening old nel was brought into camp paid $7 for cost and trouble of finding her. Wm & Amanda sick. . . . watered our cattle at the well springs poor water at that . . . .

Oct 5:

Drove 12 miles and camped without water or wood plenty of people a begging for brew and mad because they did not get it. . . . drove . . . passed a spring about noon, the spring being verry weak we give them only one bucket of water to each yoke and camped on John days river at the spring we saw Whisler he met us and that was the first we had seen of him since we was at Salmon falls, he was in pursuit of his gray mare which he said had been stolen from him, he said that he had been informed at the Dalles that we were some distance behind and was about

out of flour, and provision and he had a sack of flour with him which he said he had brought it on purpose for us, but luckily as it happened that we had plenty of flour and provision. . . .

Oct 11:

Remained in camp til late Arminda ann Vanbuskirk died we buried her on the left hand sie of the road on the side hill 1 mile from John Days river and then drove 8 miles and camped . . . . Drove 20 miles and camped on the Columbia river This is the biggest drive that we have made for 1 month. . . .

Oct 18:

Remained in camp Sold our oxen $50.00 per yoke all around . . . Loadedup and started on the pack trail with Whislers mare and Father. . . . At the Cascades . . . at the steamboat landing below the Cascades . . . Renewed the trip on the trail

Oct 29:

Arrived at Portland

Oct 30:

Went to Oregon city

Oct 31:

Remained in the city

INDEX

This is a person-name-only index. Content within the preface, appendix, and bibliography is not included. A superscript number is used to disambiguate persons of the same name, as explained on pages xvi and xvii. An **f**, **p**, or **ch** appended to a page number indicates a **f**igure, **p**ortrait, or genealogical **ch**art. Underscores (_____) replace an unknown first or last name. The maiden name of a married woman is enclosed in parentheses, as is the surname of each previous husband.

A

Able
  Martha, 107
  May, 107
Alexander, I. H., 22**f**
Anderson, Laurence, 14
  See also Van Buskirk, Laurens[1] Andriessen
Andriessen, Laurens[1], 6–7, 9, 10**f**, 11, 68. *See also* Van Buskirk, Laurens[1] Andriessen
Arentszen, Fredrick, 11
Arnett, A. C., 76, 122
Ashton(?), Sarah/Sarah Suzannah, v**ch**, 29, 102**ch**

B

Barentsen
  Barents/Barent Christian, 12, 20
  Christian, 9–12
  Jannetje (Jans), v**ch**, 11–17, 20, 23, 108**ch**
Barlow, Sam, 91
Barnum, P. T., 107
Baylis
  Harriet Maria, iv**ch**
  Maria Jerusha (Roberts), iv**ch**
  Samuel French, iv**ch**
Benezet, Phillip, 30
Blackmore, Marie/Mary, 92, 102**ch**
Borckeloo, Annetje Janse, 22

Braisted, Todd W., 82
Brickers, Margritie (Van der Linde), 23, 104
Brown, *family,* 57–58, 58**f**
Buckman, Mary, v**ch**
Buzzkirk/Buskirk/Boskirk, 1
 See also Van Buskirk

C

Campbell, Maria, 105, 108**ch**
Carstensen, Claas "The Norman," 12
Carteret
 Governor Philip, 12, 14
 Lady Elizabeth, 14
Cellars
 family, 48, 52
 James, 52
 Joseph, 53
 Mary[7] (Van Buskirk), 53
Charles II, King of England, 36
Clark, William, 88
Cline
 George S., 58
 Rebecca (Pitters) (Van Buskirk), 57–58
Collier, Volkertie, 23, 104, 108**ch**
Cramer, Zadoc, 39
Cree, Anne Elizabeth, 47, 52, 77, 122

D

Davis, Jefferson, 107
De Draijer/de Drayer, Laurens, 10
 See also Van Buskirk, Laurens[1] Andriessen
Deming
 Clara (_____), iv**ch**
 David Crawford "Ford," iv**ch**
 Donal, iv**ch**
 Dorothy Elizabeth, iv**ch**, 73, 80**ch**, 102**ch**, 119**ch**, 121, 124**p**
 Harriet Maria (Baylis), iv**ch**
De Rapelje/de Rapelje
 Catalina/Catalyntie (Trico), 3–4, 6, 26
 Elisabett, v**ch**, 6, 26
 Gaspard Colet, 3–4
 Joris, 3–4, 6, 26
 Sarah, 4, 6, 26
Devin, Augustus, 116
Dickinson, Philemon, 85
"Doc Holiday", 125
Doeding, Louise, iv**ch**
Donck. *See* Van der Donck
Doyle, Arthur Conan, 131
Draijer/Drayer/Droyer, 10
 See also Van Buskirk, Laurens[1] Andriessen
Dr. Van. *See* Van Buskirk, Edmund[10] Linford

E

Edsell, Samuel, 21
Edwards, Matilda Emily, 119**ch**
Eldridge
    Arminda[8ot], 99
    Sarah[7ot], 99, 102**ch**
Elliott
    family, 48, 52
    Aaron, 50, 52
    Mary Ann, 50, 110, 119**ch**
Evans, Margaret I., 92–93, 99, 102**ch**

F

Fairman, D., 34**f**
Fairweather
    Antje[4] (Van Buskirk), 26–27
    John, 27
Finley, *family*, 48
Firestone, William, 51
Flint, Rosalie Viola (Matthews), 45
Forrest
    Audrey Elizabeth (Van Buskirk), 80**ch**, 130**f**, 132, 133**f**, 134**ch**
    Hugh, 80**ch**, 134**ch**
Friedman, Ephraim, 128–130, 128**f**

G

Gaston, Joseph, 103**p**
Gilliam, Cornelius, 96
Gray
    family, 48, 112
    Mary Jane, 112–114, 116, 117**f**, 119**ch**
    Robert, 112
Gregory, John, 30
Gresley
    Ella[9] Florilla (Van Buskirk), 61–62, 61**f**, 63**f**
    Leo, 62
Grevenraedt, Anna, 19
Gullung
    Charles Michael "Charlie" (b. 2005), 80**ch**, 133**f**, 134**ch**
    Charles William, 80**ch**, 133**f**, 134**ch**
    John Henry "Hank," 80**ch**, 133**f**, 134**ch**
    Noah William, 80**ch**, 133**f**, 134**ch**
    Sarah Lynn (Van Buskirk), 55, 57, 80**ch**, 130**f**, 132, 133**f**, 134**ch**
    Violet Henrietta, 80**ch**, 133**f**, 134**ch**
    Walter Edward Lueck, 80**ch**, 133**f**, 134**ch**

H

Hardesty, H. H., 49**f**, 51

Harmeanse
  Hans, 20–21
  Trientie/Catherine, 20–22
  Willemtje (Warnaers) (Van Borckeloo), 20

Harrison
  Benjamin, 116
  John, 116
  John Scott, 116
  William Henry, 116

Henderson, Sarah (Sloane), 101**f**, 102**ch**

Himes, George H., 103**p**

Hoaglandt
  Dirck Cornelissen, v**ch**
  Elisabett (De Rapelje/de Rapelje), v**ch**, 6, 26

Holiday, "Doc," 125

Hoochlandt/Hogeland, Marytie, v**ch**, 26–27

Hoochlandt/Hooglandt
  Catherine (Richou), v**ch**
  Joris Dirckse, v**ch**

Hopkins, G. M., 15**f**, 25**f**

Howells, William White, 126, 130

Hudson, Henry, 3, 4, 5**f**

Huff, Dulcena, 95, 102**ch**

Hunt, Katherine, 52

I

Isenberger
  Mary Belle (Van Buskirk), 111, 119**ch**
  Samuel, 119**ch**

J

Jans, Jannetje, v**ch**, 11–17, 20, 23, 108**ch**

Jansen
  Joseph Edward, 80**ch**
  Kathleen Elizabeth (Treacy), 80**ch**
  Leo Tracy, 80**ch**
  Mark Edward, 80**ch**

Johnson
  family, 33, 35
  Catherine, 35, 46–47
  Nicholas, 35
  Sarah[5] (Van Buskirk), 30, 34–35

Johnston, John, 23

Jones, Wilbur D., Jr., 106**p**

Index

K

Kieft, William, 12
Knouse
  family, 60, 63**f**
  Aaron L., 61–62
  D, 60
  Daniel, iv**ch**, 61
  David S., 62
  Francis, iv**ch**
  Mary/Maria, iv**ch**, 60–63, 61**f**, 63**f**, 102**ch**, 119**ch**
  Mary/Maria (Sterner), iv**ch**, 61
Kopp, Peter, 105

L

Lackey, Howard L., 32, 35, 36, 41
Laudahn
  Ethel[9] May (Van Buskirk), 62, 63**f**
  Frank, 62
"Laurens the Drawer", 10
  See also Van Buskirk, Laurens[1] Andriessen
Levers, Mary, 42, 46
Lewis
  Meriwether, 88
  S., 34**f**
Linn, Jane, 30
Little, Jerusha, 105, 108**ch**

Lueck, Bette Jo, 77, 80**ch**, 102**ch**, 119**ch**, 127, 130**f**, 132, 133**f**, 134**ch**
Lydgate
  Alexander Edmund "Alex," 80**ch**, 133**f**, 134**ch**
  Audrey Elizabeth (Van Buskirk), 80**ch**, 130**f**, 132, 133**f**, 134**ch**
  Christopher John "Chris," 80**ch**, 133**f**, 134**ch**
  Theodore Edmund "Theo," 80**ch**, 133**f**, 134**ch**

M

Mattes, Merrill J., 93, 95–96
Matthews, Rosalie Viola, 45
McKee
  family, 48, 52
  Mary Ann, 48–49
"The Miller of Ramapos", 83
Mills, Hannah, 52–53
Minuet, Peter, 6
More, Nicholas, 27
Morrow
  Ann "Annie," iv**ch**, 55–57, 60, 102**ch**, 119**ch**
  Jane, 55
Muterspaug, Sandra Jean, 80**ch**

N

Neighbors, Elizabeth, 49
Nelson, William, 10, 13**f**, 22**f**, 35

O

O'Sullivan, John, 88

P

Penn, William, 27
Perry, Elias H., 95–96
Pitters, Rebecca, 57–58
Pomerene, Joel, 112–113
Pursell, Cristiana, v**ch**

R

Rapelje. *See* De Rapelje/de Rapelje
Richardson, Sarah, 47
Richou, Catherine, v**ch**
Riley, Elmira, 119**ch**
Roberts, Maria Jerusha, iv**ch**
Rulon, Mary, 93–95, 102**ch**

S

Sabine, Lorenzo, 82
Schaphorst, Sophie, iv**ch**
Schilling, Robert, 40
Schomp, *family*, 23
Schwarze
    Henry, iv**ch**
    Louise (Doeding), iv**ch**
    Mary/Maria Louise, iv**ch**, 68–70, 69**f**, 70**f**, 78**p**, 102**ch**, 119**ch**
    Sophie (Schaphorst), iv**ch**
    William, iv**ch**
Shaw
    family, 30
    Richard, 30
Shoemaker, Irene, 18, 20, 23, 29, 40, 44–45, 66, 68, 110
Sloane, Sarah, 101**f**, 102**ch**
Smith, Esther, iv**ch**
Snyder, _____, 98
Sterner
    family, 62, 63**f**
    Casper, 61
    Daniel, iv**ch**
    Esther (Smith), iv**ch**
    Mary/Maria, iv**ch**, 61
Stevens
    Jack, 80**ch**
    Nancy[11] Louise (Van Buskirk) (Treacy), 68, 75, 80**ch**, 102**ch**, 121, 124**p**

Strawn/Straughan
   family, 33
   Anne[6] (Van Buskirk), 46–47
   Cristiana (Pursell), v**ch**
   George, 46–47
   Jacob, v**ch**, 45–46
   Jacob II, 35, 46
   John, 45–46
   Lancelot, v**ch**, 45
   Mary, v**ch**, 42, 44, 45, 102**ch**
   Mary (Buckman), v**ch**
   Mary[6] (Van Buskirk), 46
   Susannah[5] (Van Buskirk), 30, 34–35, 46
   Thomas, 45–46

Stuyvesant, Peter, 11

Sweatland, Rosemary Brown, 80**ch**

Swinand
   Andrew John, 80**ch**
   Georgia Elizabeth, 80**ch**
   Laura Elizabeth (Tanner), 80**ch**
   Tanner John, 80**ch**

T

Tanner
   James Wallace, 80**ch**, 102**ch**
   Joan[11] Elizabeth (Van Buskirk), 33, 75, 80**ch**, 102**ch**, 121, 124**p**, 131
   Laura Elizabeth, 80**ch**

"The Miller of Ramapos", 83

Théry
   Amy Louise (Van Buskirk), 80**ch**, 130**f**, 132, 133**f**, 134**ch**
   Benjamin Franck Emile, 80**ch**, 133**f**, 134**ch**
   François Etienne, 80**ch**, 133**f**, 134**ch**
   Nicolas Edmund, 80**ch**, 133**f**, 134**ch**

Treacy
   Cole Patrick, 80**ch**
   Connor Edmund, 80**ch**
   James Neal, 80**ch**
   James William, 80**ch**, 102**ch**
   Kathleen Elizabeth, 80**ch**
   Kevin James, 80**ch**
   Mariah Jean, 80**ch**
   Michael J., 80**ch**
   Nancy[11] Louise (Van Buskirk), 68, 75, 80**ch**, 102**ch**, 121, 124**p**
   Rosemary Brown (Sweatland), 80**ch**
   Sandra Jean (Muterspaug), 80**ch**

Trico, Catalina/Catalyntie, 3–4, 6, 26

V

Van Barkeloo, Catherine Hanse, 83

Van Boeskerksp/vonBuschkirk, 9
See also Van Buskirk

Van Booskirk/Van Boskerck, 1
See also Van Buskirk

Van Borckeloo
  Harmen, 20
  Willemtje (Warnaers), 20

Van Burskirk/Van Bursick/ VanBuskirk, 1. See also Van Buskirk

Van Buskirk
  family, 1, 9, 12, 23, 32–36, 39, 52, 94
  Aaron[8r] Elliott "A. E.," 50, 65**f**, 77, 110–118, 111**p**, 117**f**, 119**ch**
  Abraham (son of Pieter[2]), 83
  Abraham[3], 23–24
  Abraham[4L], 84–86
  Abraham[5L], 83
  Alice[10] Louise, 68, 78**p**, 118
  Amelia[6], 42
  Amy Louise, 80**ch**, 130**f**, 132, 133**f**, 134**ch**
  Andrew (b. 1778), 45, 92
  Andrew[3L], 82
  Andrew[4] (b.1719), 26–27, 29
  Andrew[5], 29–30, 42
  Andrew[7ot] (b. 1827), 93–101, 94**f**, 101**f**, 102**ch**, 103**p**, 121, 139–148
  Andries[2], v**ch**, 12, 18–20, 23, 25**f**, 26–27, 32, 40, 82, 104
  Andries[3], 19
  Anna (Grevenraedt), 19
  Anna (Weis), 29
  Anna[3], 19
  Ann "Annie" (Morrow), iv**ch**, 55–57, 60, 102**ch**, 119**ch**
  Anne[6], 46–47
  Anne Elizabeth (Cree), 47, 52, 77, 122
  Antje[4], 26–27
  Arminda[8ot] (Eldridge), 99
  Audrey Elizabeth, 80**ch**, 130**f**, 132, 133**f**, 134**ch**
  Benjamin[3L], 83
  Bess "Bessie," 117**f**, 118, 121
  Bette Jo (Lueck), 77, 80**ch**, 102**ch**, 119**ch**, 127, 130**f**, 132, 133**f**, 134**ch**
  "Blue Ike"/Isaac[6d], 106
  Catherine. See Trientie/Catherine (Harmeanse)
  Catherine (Johnson), 35, 46–47
  Catherine[5], 46
  Catherine Hanse (Van Barkeloo), 83
  Charity (Van Horn), 27
  Charles[6], 42, 46, 48–49
  Christiana[6], 42
  Daniel[4] (b. 1736), 26–27
  Daniel[5], 29–31, 42

Index

Daniel⁷ᵒᵗ (b. 1833), 102**ch**
David⁶ᵈ, 105–108, 106**p**, 108**ch**, 121
Dorothy Elizabeth (Deming), iv**ch**, 73, 80**ch**, 102**ch**, 119**ch**, 121, 124**p**
"Dr. Van." *See* Edmund¹⁰ Linford
Dulcena (Huff), 95, 102**ch**
Edmund⁹ Michael (b. 1875), 50, 55, 62–63, 63**f**, 64–72, 65**f**, 66**f**, 67**f**, 69**f**, 70**f**, 71**p**, 72**p**, 77, 102**ch**, 119**ch**, 130, 131
Edmund¹⁰ Linford "Dr. Van" (b. 1907), iv**ch**, 68, 73–80, 78**p**, 79**p**, 80**ch**, 102**ch**, 119**ch**, 121–123, 123**p**, 124**p**, 128**f**, 130–131, 131
Edmund¹¹ Michael (b. 1941), iv**ch**, 33, 55, 57, 75, 80**ch**, 102**ch**, 119**ch**, 120–132, 123**p**, 124**p**, 127**p**, 128**f**, 130**f**, 132**p**, 133**f**, 134**ch**
Elizabeth (Neighbors), 49
Elizabeth⁷ (b. 1825), 50
Elizabeth⁸ (b. 1850), 56
Ella⁹ Florilla, 61–62, 61**f**, 63**f**
Ellenora⁸, 56
Elmira (Riley), 119**ch**
Ethel⁹ May, 62, 63**f**
Etta⁸, 57
Fytje³, 19
Geertru, 23
George⁴ (b. 1721), v**ch**, 26–31, 33, 42, 46, 82, 92, 102**ch**, 121
George⁶ (b. 1767), 93–95, 102**ch**
George⁶ Levers, 42
George⁷ (b. 1813), 50, 55
George⁸ (b. 1843), 56, 59**p**, 121
Helena³, 19
Hendrickje (Van der Linde), 20, 82
Isaac³, 24
Isaac⁴ᵈ (b. 1760), 105, 108**ch**
Isaac⁵ᵈ, 105
Isaac⁶ᵈ "Blue Ike," 106
Jacob⁵ᴸ, 84–85
Jacob⁷ʳ (b. 1825), 41, 50, 55, 109–110, 119**ch**
Jacobus³, 84
Jacobus³ Pietersen, 83
James³ᴸ (b. 1704), 85–86
James⁴ᴸ, 86
James⁵ᵈ (b. 1796), 105, 108**ch**
James⁷ (b. 1811), iv**ch**, 41, 46, 49–50, 54–59, 56**f**, 58**f**, 59**p**, 60, 102**ch**, 109–110, 119**ch**
Jan³. *See* John³/Jan/Johannes
Jan³ᴸ. *See* John³ᴸ/Jan
Jane (Morrow), 55
Jannetje (Jans) (Barentsen), v**ch**, 11–17, 20, 23, 108**ch**
Jannetje (Van der Linde), v**ch**, 19
Jannetje⁴ (b. 1714), 26–27
Jemima (Wynkoop), 27

157

Van Buskirk *continued*
- Jemima[8] (b. 1856), 56
- Jerusha (Little), 105, 108**ch**
- Joan[11] Elizabeth, 33, 75, 80**ch**, 102**ch**, 121, 124**p**, 131
- Johannes[3] (son of Andries[2]) *See* John[3]/Jan/Johannes
- Johannis[3] (bap. 1694) (son of Thomas[2]), 23–25
- John[3]/Jan/Johannes (b. ca. 1670s), v**ch**, 6, 19, 26–28, 28**f**, 29, 32–33, 81–82
- John[3L]/Jan, 82–83
- John[4], 83–84
- John[5] (b. 1745), 29–30, 42, 44, 45, 92, 102**ch**
- John[6d] "Sandy," 106
- John[7] (b. 1789, son of George[6]), 95, 102**ch**
- John[7] (son of Joseph[6]), 55
- John[7ot] (b. 1818), 101, 101**f**, 102**ch**
- John Wesley (b. 1853), 111, 119**ch**
- Joost[3]/Joseph, 19, 26–28
- Joost[3L], 82
- Joseph (son of Jacob[7r]), 111, 112, 119**ch**
- Joseph[5] (b. 1751), 29–30, 34, 42–47, 92, 96, 102**ch**
- Joseph[6] (b. 1782), iv**ch**, v**ch**, 30, 41–53, 102**ch**, 109, 119**ch**
- Joseph[6b] (b. 1776), 44–45, 92
- Joseph[8] (b. 1844), 33, 50, 56–57, 59**p**, 77, 111–112, 119**ch**, 121
- Joseph T.[7ot] (b. 1824), 98, 102**ch**
- Lafayette[8ot], 101**f**
- Laurens[1] Andriessen (b. 1625), v**ch**, 7, 9–17, 13**f**, 15**f**, 16**f**, 20, 23, 25**f**, 26, 32, 35, 68, 104, 108**ch**, 120
- Laurens[2] (b. 1660-1666), 12, 18, 20, 82–83, 86
- Laurens[3]/Lawrence, 19
- Laurens[3L] "The Miller of Ramapos," 83
- Laurens[3] Pietersen, 83
- Laurens[4L] Jansen, 83
- Lawrence (son of John[5]), 44
- Lawrence[4], 83
- Lawrence[4L] Jacobus, 85–86
- Lawrence[5]/Lawson[5], 29–30, 34–35, 41, 42, 46–47
- Lawrence[6] (son of Lawrence[5]), 46–47
- Lawson[4]/Lawrence[4] (Captain), 40–41
- Linford[8], iv**ch**, 50, 57, 58, 59**p**, 60–63, 61**f**, 62**p**, 63**f**, 102**ch**, 111**p**, 119**ch**
- Lucy Ann[6d] (Van Buskirk), 105, 107, 108**ch**
- Luke Edmund, 80**ch**, 130**f**, 133**f**, 134**ch**

Lynford⁶, 42, 46, 49
Margaret I. (Evans), 92–93, 99, 102**ch**
Margritie (Van der Linde) (Brickers), 23, 104
Maria (Campbell), 105, 108**ch**
Marie/Mary (Blackmore), 92, 102**ch**
Martha (Able), 107
Mary (_____), 95
Mary (Levers), 42, 46
Mary (Rulon), 93–95, 102**ch**
Mary (Strawn), v**ch**, 42, 44, 45, 102**ch**
Mary⁴ᵈ, 105
Mary⁶, 46
Mary⁷, 53
Mary⁸ᵒᵗ, 98–99
Mary Ann (Elliott), 50, 110, 119**ch**
Mary Ann (McKee), 48–49
Mary Belle, 111, 119**ch**
Mary Jane (Gray), 112–114, 116, 117**f**, 119**ch**
Mary/Maria (Knouse), iv**ch**, 60–63, 61**f**, 63**f**, 102**ch**, 119**ch**
Mary/Maria (Vandeventer), 104–105, 108**ch**
Mary/Maria Louise (Schwarze), iv**ch**, 68–70, 69**f**, 70**f**, 78**p**, 102**ch**, 119**ch**
Marytie (Hoochlandt/Hogeland), v**ch**, 26–27
Matilda Emily (Edwards), 119**ch**
May (Able), 107
Michael³/³ᵈ (b. 1721), 24, 104–105, 108**ch**
Moses⁵, 29–30
Mrs. (wife of Abraham⁴ᴸ), 85
Mrs. (wife of Capt. Van Buskirk), 40–41
Nancy¹¹ Louise (b. 1931), 68, 75, 80**ch**, 102**ch**, 121, 124**p**
Nicholas⁶ (b. 1781), 46–47
Otis⁹ Walter, 61–63, 61**f**, 63**f**, 71**p**
Peter⁴, 83–84
Pieter² (b. 1666), 12, 15**f**, 17, 18–23, 21**f**, 22**f**, 82–83, 86
Pieter³, 24
Pieter⁴, 83
Rachel⁸, 57
Rebecca (_____), 41
Rebecca (Pitters), 57–58
Rebecca (Villars), iv**ch**, 45–46, 49–50, 51, 54–55, 102**ch**, 109, 119**ch**
Robert⁶, 42
Ruth⁸, 57
Samuel⁴ (bap. 1716), 26–27
"Sandy"/John⁶ᵈ, 106
Sarah (_____), v**ch**, 29, 102**ch**
Sarah (Richardson), 47

Van Buskirk *continued*
   Sarah (Sloane) (Henderson), 101**f**, 102**ch**
   Sarah[5], 30, 34–35
   Sarah[7ot], 97, 100–101, 102**ch**
   Sarah[7ot] (Eldridge), 99, 102**ch**
   Sarah[8], 56
   Sarah Lynn (b. 1972), 55, 57, 80**ch**, 130**f**, 132, 133**f**, 134**ch**
   Sarah/Sarah Suzannah (Ashton?), v**ch**, 29, 102**ch**
   Susannah[5], 30, 34–35, 46
   Theodosa (_____), 83
   Thomas[2] (b. 1668), 12, 17, 18–20, 23–24, 24**f**, 25**f**, 40, 82, 86, 104, 108**ch**
   Trientie/Catherine (Harmeanse), 20–22
   Volkertie (Collier), 23, 104, 108**ch**
   William, 94
   William (b. 1822), 102**ch**
   William[6], 42
   William[6ot] (b.1789), 33, 41, 44–45, 92–95, 100–101, 101**f**, 102**ch**, 103**p**, 110
   William[7], 95
   William[8], 95

VanBuskirk. *See* Van Buskirk
van Crieckenbeeck, Daniel, 6
Van der Donck, Adriaen, 5**f**
Van der Linde
   Fytje (Van Gelder), v**ch**, 19, 20
   Hendrickje, 20, 82
   Jannetje, v**ch**, 19
   Joost, v**ch**, 19, 20
   Margritie, 23, 104
Vandeventer, Mary/Maria, 104–105, 108**ch**
Van Gelder, Fytje, v**ch**, 19, 20
Van Hoorn
   Christian Barentsen, 9–12
   Jannetje (Jans), v**ch**, 11–17, 20, 23, 108**ch**
Van Horn, Charity, 27
Van Swartensluys, Fredrick Arentszen, 11
Verhuls, Willem, 6
Villars
   John, 45, 46
   Rebecca, iv**ch**, 45–46, 49–50, 51, 54–55, 102**ch**, 109, 119**ch**
Vreeland, Hartman Claesen, 21

W

Wald, George, 126
Warnaers, Willemtje, 20
Washington, George, 82, 84–85
Watson, James, 126
Weis, Anna, 29
Whisler
   Elijah, 97, 100–101
   Sarah[7ot] (Van Buskirk), 97, 100–101, 102**ch**
Wilt, Fred, 125–126, 130
Winfield, Charles H., 13**f**, 18, 22**f**
Wither, William, 45
Wynkoop
   family, 27
   Garret, 27, 28**f**
   Jemima, 27

Y

Young, _____, 95

Z

Zabriske, Albert, 23

Unknown Surname

Clara, iv**ch**
Mary, 95
Rebecca, 41
Sarah, v**ch**, 29, 102**ch**
Theodosa, 83

www.ingramcontent.com/pod-product-compliance
Lightning Source LLC
Chambersburg PA
CBHW040844100426
42812CB00014B/2605